"One of the many wise things my mom taught me at an early age was to count my blessings. She helped me look around and be thankful for all the things most of us take for granted on a daily basis. It was life-enhancing advice. Now along comes Kevin Carroll with this wonderful book that adds to my mom's wisdom. He reminds us over and over, in a friendly and humble manner, that gratitude is at the foundation of a good life. Read it — and count your blessing along the way."

Hal Urban
Author, *Life's Greatest Lessons* and *Positive Words, Powerful Results*

"Kevin Carroll's reminders have helped me resist the urge to complain and replace it with an appreciation of all that I have. *A Moment's Pause for Gratitude* can be read in one sitting or used as a daily prayer of thanks; either way, it serves as an antidote to negativity and an aide for the peaceful mind. I expect it will be as helpful to other readers as it has been for me and I'm grateful to him for putting it into this world."

Roland Merullo
Author, *Breakfast with Buddha* and *The Delight of Being Ordinary*

"The more I read the entries in this collection, the more I wanted to read them again, and again. Kevin Carroll's ability to grapple with what is of value along the paths of life and chance reveal in him a heart that is energized by gratitude. Sometimes I couldn't put his writing down. At other times, reading one entry was all that mattered. Then again, I'd be drawn back to his collection hoping that my eyes could see the way he sees… with his heart. The experience he offers us will give you goose bumps because he repeatedly touches upon what really matters."

Rev. Richard Hilliard
Priest of the Diocese of San José, California

A
MOMENT'S PAUSE
for
GRATITUDE

Enrich Your Life with a Focus on Gratitude

Kevin Carroll

KEVIN CARROLL

BALBOA.
PRESS

A DIVISION OF HAY HOUSE

Balboa Press books may be ordered through booksellers or by contacting:

Balboa Press
A Division of Hay House
1663 Liberty Drive
Bloomington, IN 47403
www.balboapress.com
1 (877) 407-4847

Print information available on the last page.

ISBN: 978-1-5043-9009-5 (sc)
ISBN: 978-1-5043-9010-1 (e)

Balboa Press rev. date: 10/12/2017

For my mother,
Peg Carroll,
with gratitude for her
unconditional love
which has consistently nourished me
throughout my lifetime.

TABLE OF CONTENTS

ACKNOWLEDGMENTS

"No act of kindness is ever wasted."
~ Aesop

Very rarely in life does anyone accomplish anything by him/herself. More often than not, our success comes as a result of the help and guidance we receive from any number of sources. The publication of *A Moment's Pause for Gratitude* is no different.

As I will mention in the *Introduction* of this book, my journey of gratitude began at the Jesuit Retreat Center in Los Altos, California in November 2006. I am grateful for the retreat facilitators and retreat center staff who made that weekend such a life-changing experience for me.

I would like to thank Roland Merullo, Hal Urban, and Don McPhail, three accomplished authors, who provided encouragement, inspiration, and guidance to me throughout the process of writing this book.

I would also like to thank Fr. Richard Hilliard, a longtime friend and a priest of the Catholic Diocese of San José, California, for his constant support and encouragement.

I am especially grateful to my family — to my three sons, Tom, Steve, and Brendan, for their unending love and support, and for their willingness to allow me to share some of their life experiences, many of which have been sources of gratitude in my life, and to my wife, Kathy, for her enduring love, encouragement, and patience. I'd also like to express my gratitude to Kathy for the countless times she has challenged me to be a better writer, a better parent, and a better person.

Finally, I would like to thank my mother, Peg Carroll, to whom this book is dedicated. For more than ten years, Mom has read, printed, and often shared my blog posts with others. The unconditional love she has provided throughout my lifetime is, and will always be, a tremendous source of gratitude for me.

And as my Dad would have said, "Thanks be to God."

INTRODUCTION

Parent: *"What do you say?"*
Child: *"Thank you!"*

One of the first lessons we learn in early childhood is one of life's most important: Gratitude. Learning to be grateful, and learning to express our gratitude to others, is more than just a basic social skill. It lays the foundation upon which we can live a happy and fulfilling life. William Arthur Ward may have said it best when he wrote, *"Feeling gratitude and not expressing it is like wrapping a present and not giving it."* Yet how many of us fail to adequately let others know how grateful we are for the ways they enrich our lives?

It's so easy to take people for granted. Similarly, it is quite easy for us to take for granted the many experiences, opportunities, and abilities with which we have been blessed. How often do we pause in gratitude for the gift of our eyesight, our ability to walk, or for the educational opportunities we've had in our lifetime? How often are we consciously grateful for the love of our parents, family members, and friends?

In November 2006, I had the opportunity to participate in a weekend retreat at the Jesuit Retreat Center in Los Altos, California. The focus of the retreat was "gratitude." I don't recall anything specific about the weekend other than the drive down the hill from the retreat center at the conclusion of the retreat on Sunday afternoon. I was absolutely overwhelmed with a sense of gratitude for the people who had enriched my life, for the opportunities

I'd experienced, and, yes, even for my ability to see, hear, smell, touch, and taste. I wondered, at that moment, how I might maintain the sense of gratitude I was experiencing. I didn't have an answer at the time.

I returned to my work as a high school teacher the next day. We were approaching the end of the first semester, with exams just a week or two away. Not surprisingly, my focus shifted from gratitude to the responsibilities of my job. It wasn't until exams had ended and our Christmas break had begun that I revisited the question about maintaining a focus on gratitude. At that point, I knew exactly what I wanted to do. On December 23rd, I created a blog.

I have always enjoyed writing. Throughout my life, I've experienced writing to be quite therapeutic for me. So the idea of beginning a blog about gratitude just made sense. I called it *Attitude of Gratitude*. For a little more than a year, from December 23, 2006 to January 1, 2008, I wrote and posted an entry every day. In the years since that time, I've written consistently, but less frequently. At the beginning of 2017, I took a month off from writing in order to review all the posts I'd written in the past ten years — approximately 1,500 in all. I deleted more than fifty entries, those which, in my opinion, were inconsistent with my theme of gratitude.

The book in your hands contains fifty posts from this blog. My hope is that, by sharing these stories with you, you will develop a greater appreciation for the benefits of living your life with a genuine attitude of gratitude. I also hope to inspire you to be more aware of the people, experiences, opportunities, and possessions in your own life for which you might be grateful. Finally, I hope to motivate you to express your gratitude, freely and frequently, to those responsible for the gifts with which you've been blessed.

Each chapter contains two or more reflection questions. If you find them to be helpful for you, please take some time to consider your responses. Fear not! There is no final exam at the end of this book.

It's been said many times that life is a journey. I invite and encourage you to enrich your journey with a focus on gratitude.

1

It's Time!

*"It is hard to fail, but it is worse
never to have tried to succeed."*
~ Theodore Roosevelt

A few things have happened recently which I simply cannot ignore —
experiences which finally pushed me off my chair of complacency. The
first was seeing the quote above by President Theodore Roosevelt, which
I happened to see posted on a friend's Facebook page. Throughout
my life, I have had a fear of failure. For this reason, there were a few
opportunities I missed out on. It took me a long time to realize that the
word "fail" is an acronym: *First Attempt In Learning.*

Another nudge came from a few lines of a book I read several years
ago. Having thoroughly enjoyed Roland Merullo's novel, <u>Breakfast
with Buddha</u>, the first of a dozen books I've read by this gifted author,
I picked up another of his books, <u>Golfing with God</u>. Something I read
toward the end of this book seemed to contain another message for me,
a message telling me that the time had come for me to take the risk and
seriously consider publishing some of my writing. In Merullo's story,
God was speaking to Herman Fins-Winston, the main character, urging
him to take on a particular golf challenge. God said, *"Imagine if Sam
Snead or Ben Hogan had never taken up golf. Deep inside their spiritual*

selves they would know what they were capable of, and they'd have to live with that gnawing, secret frustration..." Ouch! That one hit home.

As if that message might not be clear enough for me, just a few days after mentioning <u>Breakfast with Buddha</u> in one of my blog posts, I was stunned when I opened my e-mail and found an unsolicited message from Roland Merullo himself. Someone who knows him apparently happened to see my blog post and sent him the link. He wrote to thank me for mentioning his book on my blog. Then, in a brief exchange of emails, he provided some encouraging feedback on my writing ability and style.

Since that time, Roland and I have continued to keep in touch. I was grateful when he sent me a copy of yet another book he'd written, <u>Demons of the Blank Page</u>, in which he discusses fifteen obstacles that keep writers from writing. I was experiencing most of these impediments in my own life as a potential writer. In his book, he offers tips on how to effectively overcome these hurdles.

I'm convinced that the things we encounter in our lives don't just happen. I honestly believe that everything we experience happens for a reason. We might not always understand the reason at the time, but I've learned that when things do happen, our task is to give serious consideration to the challenge or opportunity being presented to us. In this case, I think the message was loud and clear.

So much for which to be grateful!

Reflection Questions:

1. Have you ever come across a quote in a book, or from some other source, which inspired you or helped to clarify a sense of direction for you?

2. What demons or impediments might be preventing you from achieving some dream you've had in your lifetime? How might you overcome these obstacles to make your dream a reality?

3. Do you agree that everything we experience in life, good or bad, happens for a reason? What life experiences influence your response to this question?

2

The Gift of Education

*"Education is the most powerful weapon
which you can use to change the world."*
~ Nelson Mandela

$\mathscr{F}$ew things open doors of opportunity as often and as effectively as a good education. Unfortunately, many high school students today are going through high school much as I did — unaware of the life-changing value of a good education. When I look back on my high school years, I can't help but realize how, in many ways, I wasted a tremendous opportunity. Fortunately, I was able to redeem myself in later years.

My experience at Saint Ignatius College Preparatory in San Francisco provided many opportunities for me to get a tremendous education. Unfortunately, my academic maturity during those years was not what one would have hoped it might be. I spent four years simply trying to get through high school, rather than consciously and conscientiously making the most of what S.I. had to offer. An opportunity lost,... but not a complete waste of time.

I managed to leave S.I. with a few things of value. I learned to write — and write well. I learned to type — and type well. Thanks to the young Jesuit priest who taught Public Speaking, I learned how to speak with confidence in front of a group. I learned, through my experience of coordinating the school's annual Christmas Food Drive for two years, that I am very capable of motivating people and organizing activities successfully. I learned to be respectful of others. My after-school volunteer experience at Helper's Home for the Mentally Retarded taught me to be compassionate towards people with disabilities. Through my experience teaching a sixth-grade religious education class at Our Lady of Mercy Parish during my senior year, I learned to both appreciate my faith and to share it freely with others. I didn't master math and science at S.I., but I certainly left the school with valuable tools which would serve me well in later years. And because of encouragement I received from several of my high school teachers, I believed in myself as a valuable human being.

Although I didn't yet have confidence in my own academic ability, after two years at a community college, one year working in the Bahamas, and part of another year exploring the possibility of a vocation to the Jesuit priesthood, I was given the opportunity to attend Santa Clara University to complete my undergraduate studies. It was there that I finally learned how to be a competent student. Despite the demands of my part-time job teaching Religious Studies and supervising dormitory students at Bellarmine College Preparatory in San José, I carried a full academic load at Santa Clara and put 100% into my studies. I learned to appreciate the opportunity I'd been given to get an excellent education. My years at S.I. had prepared me well for the challenges I faced at Santa Clara, particularly my ability to write with confidence.

My post-graduate years at the University of San Francisco were equally rewarding. I was fortunate to be part of the *Institute for Catholic Educational Leadership* and earn my Master's Degree. By that point in my life, I had developed a genuine desire to learn. I appreciate the many professors who shared their knowledge and expertise with me, most notably, Father Patrick Duffy, who challenged me to improve my critical thinking skills in his School Law course.

Yes, education is a gift. Like most gifts, we can take it or leave it. It took me awhile to understand this, but the academic struggles of my early years definitely made me a better, more compassionate teacher. I will always be tremendously grateful for the gift of my education.

Reflection Questions:

1. What do you believe is the key to success in life?

2. What were some of the most valuable lessons you learned in the classroom setting?

3. Was there one teacher, in particular, who encouraged you and motivated you to challenge yourself to achieve beyond your own expectations? How did s/he do this?

3

The Gift of Challenging Times

*"Hardships often prepare ordinary people
for an extraordinary destiny."*
~ C.S. Lewis

In some ways, I often feel that my life has been fairly easy — too easy, perhaps. I've been blessed with a wonderful family and some amazing friends. I received an outstanding education. I was gainfully employed for forty years doing what I felt called to do and what I enjoyed doing. I've always had a comfortable place to call home. I've been blessed with multiple opportunities to travel overseas. I've never been deprived of anything I truly needed. I'm tremendously grateful for all these undeserved gifts, but I also appreciate some of the difficult experiences I've endured in my lifetime.

I had a little trouble learning to manage my money when I was in elementary school. My mother, however, taught me a difficult, but valuable life lesson one day in the summer of 1966. I was twelve-years-old at the time. I wanted to purchase some plastic golf balls so that I could practice my golf swing in the backyard of a home we were house-sitting in Monterey, California. Mom took me to *Sir Discount*, a local store with a small sports department. I found a bag of a dozen balls for something like $3.50. When Mom suggested that we should look

9

around at other stores to see if we could get a better deal, I assured her, as only a twelve-year-old can, that I was absolutely certain that this was a good price for the bag of balls, so I bought them. A few days later, we happened to be in another store. Mom led me to the sports department of that store, where we found a bag of eighteen plastic golf balls, similar in quality to the ones I had purchased, for about a dollar less. Point made! I can honestly say that I've never had money-management issues since that time. It was a lesson well-learned.

During my middle school years, I had some social skills issues. I related exceptionally well with adults at that time in my life, but, for some reason, I struggled getting along with some of my peers. My seventh and eighth grade years were painful, to say the least. Despite the challenges of those years, I learned some valuable lessons about social cruelty and what motivates some kids to act the way they do. I am confident that these lessons made me a better person — and a better teacher. During my forty years as an educator, I was much more aware of, and compassionate towards, the marginalized students in my classroom than I might have been had I never experienced being one of them. I was able to use what I learned in middle school to teach acceptance, empathy, and respect among my students.

I struggled academically, too. From about sixth grade through my first two years of college, school was a challenge for me. I know that much of the difficulty I experienced was due to a lack of academic maturity, but I also never mastered effective study skills until I was a student at Santa Clara University. I'm not saying that those skills were never taught. I'm simply acknowledging the fact that I didn't absorb them at the appropriate time! The fact that school was difficult for me also made me a much better teacher. I knew how it felt to struggle. I was quite familiar with the feeling of stress associated with not meeting academic expectations or not comprehending a particular concept. I knew all too well the frustration of sitting through a test knowing that I was inadequately prepared to do well on it. Being aware of these things motivated me to work patiently and compassionately with my students who were experiencing some of these same difficulties themselves.

No one wants to go through difficult times, but I've learned that such experiences are inevitable. They are also tremendous learning opportunities. It is for this reason that, in retrospect, I am grateful for them. I would not be the person I am today had I not struggled through these challenging times. It is imperative that we allow the difficulties we encounter in life to make us better, not bitter.

Reflection Questions:

1. What challenges did you overcome in your lifetime which, looking back, you realize helped you to grow into the person you are today?

2. Are there difficult times you endured in your lifetime which left you feeling bitter, rather than better? If so, is it possible, at this point, to look back at these experiences through the lens of gratitude?

4

Lifelong Learning

"There is no end to education.
It is not that you read a book,
pass an examination, and finish with education.
The whole of life, from the moment you are born
to the moment you die, is a process of learning."
~ J. Krishnamurti

My first full-time teaching job was at Saint Augustine's College in Nassau, Bahamas in the 1974-75 academic year. At that time, copies of handouts and tests were made on a hand-cranked mimeograph machine. None of the classrooms had televisions. If we needed a cassette tape player, we could borrow one from the library. Movies, should a teacher decide to show one, required a large projector for the reel-to-reel film. Technology? That was pretty much it. Things have certainly changed!!!

By the time I retired from teaching in June 2015, every student and teacher in my school had a laptop computer to use. The school provided wireless internet access throughout the campus. Classrooms were equipped with a television, VCR/DVD player, a projector for PowerPoint presentations, and a wireless printer. With all this technology, teaching strategies were quite different than what I had experienced forty years earlier.

One thing I realized as I got older is that learning is a lifelong process. I vividly recall driving home in my light blue, 1972 Volkswagen bug after my last final exam at Santa Clara University. I remember thinking that I never had to take another test again, and in fact, my role as a learner was over. Wrong!

With each new year, I continued to learn so much about teaching, relationships, finances, faith, and life in general. In terms of teaching, I was constantly learning new techniques and strategies to make me a better educator. I attended countless professional development events to keep current in the best teaching practices of the day.

Lifelong learning is necessary in most professions, I would think. Certainly, I would not want to go to a dentist who practiced dentistry the way it was practiced in the 1960's. There are so many new innovations which make dentistry more effective and less painful. The art of teaching is no different.

Even as I approached my retirement, I embraced opportunities to learn new strategies to make me more effective with the students. It would have been easy to just continue doing things the way I'd always done them, but I couldn't do that. My students expected more — and deserved more.

I'm grateful for the many opportunities I have, even in my retirement, to continue learning. Lifelong learning is essential to both personal growth and relevance in an ever-changing world. There is great wisdom in the Japanese proverb: *"If you understand everything, you must be misinformed."*

Reflection Questions:

1. In what ways have you continued to learn long after your formal classroom education ended?

2. How has the concept of lifelong learning made a positive difference in your life, personally or professionally?

5

The Gift of Solitude

"In solitude there is healing.
Speak to your soul. Listen to your heart.
Sometimes, in the absence of noise,
we find the answers."
~ Dodinsky

There is a significant difference between being "lonely" and being "alone." I'm not lonely. I am very fortunate to have many good people in my life. In fact, maybe because I have so many people in my life, and because I'm blessed with the opportunity to spend so much time with these people, I have come to a greater appreciation of being alone — of the gift of solitude.

Solitude truly is a gift. Solitude, to me, means being alone by choice, rather than by chance. Such time alone offers me the opportunity to think, to pray, to read, to write, and to dream. It's something I need, perhaps even more than I realize.

I guess I value solitude for the same reason people value good art, exotic jewelry, or hand-crafted furniture — it's rare. Throughout much of my life, I didn't get much time to be alone. Being married, raising three boys, teaching five classes of students each day, and living in a sixty-unit condominium community in the heavily-populated Silicon Valley, all made finding solitude quite a challenge. I literally had to seek it, schedule it, or get away to truly experience it. Opportunities to do this didn't arise every day.

So where did I find solitude in those busy days? Well,... sometimes I would go for a walk at 5:00 in the morning or at 10:00 at night. I didn't run into too many people then! At other times I would get on my ten-speed bike and ride along the Los Gatos Creek Trail up to the old Jesuit Novitiate in Los Gatos, where I would sit in a comfortable chair overlooking the Santa Clara Valley. In the warm weather months, I would often head out to the jacuzzi in our condominium complex after dinner, where I was able to enjoy a little peace and quiet. Occasionally, I would take a "mental health day" from work to recharge my batteries. And a few times, I managed to get away from it all — a few days in Newport Beach, a week in the Bahamas (courtesy of frequent flyer miles), or a weekend at the Jesuit Retreat Center in Los Altos. Whatever it took, wherever I could find it, I needed occasional periods of solitude in my life.

I'm retired now, so I am blessed with a fair amount of solitude. When I'm alone, I have time to give serious, prayerful consideration to all the people and things I'm truly grateful for in my life. When I'm alone, I can often better experience the presence of God. It is in these times when I become overwhelmed with what the Jesuit poet, Gerard Manley Hopkins, referred to as *"...the grandeur of God."*

Reflection Questions:

1. Do you have a sufficient amount of solitude in your life?

2. Where do you find solitude when you seek it?

3. What obstacles exist in your life which prevent you from finding the solitude you need? How can you effectively overcome these obstacles?

6

It Happens Sometimes

"It seems to me that we often,
almost sulkily, reject the good that God offers us,
because at the moment, we expected some other good."
~ C. S. Lewis

$\mathcal{C}$. S. Lewis was born in 1898. He is well known for his writings, which include such titles as <u>The Screwtape Letters</u>, <u>Mere Christianity</u>, <u>The Chronicles of Narnia</u>, and <u>Surprised by Joy</u>. The quote above, from one of his lesser-known books, <u>Letters to Malcolm: Chiefly on Prayer</u>, caused me to stop and think.

Isn't it amazing how our expectations can blind us at times? We sometimes get stuck focusing on one particular thing we want, only to fail to notice other gifts that come our way. This is another important life lesson I shared with my students during my teaching years.

Over and over again, students were urged to set goals for themselves and to be giving thoughtful consideration to their future. Few people, however, seemed to be reminding them to be attentive to today. The process of goal-setting definitely has its value. We need goals. It's often said, *"If you don't know where you're going, there's a pretty good chance you'll never get there."* I, too, encouraged my students to set goals and to plan for their future, but not at the expense of overlooking what was happening in their lives each and every day.

So often, people desire things, ask for things, or even pray for things. Then, with great anticipation, they focus their full attention on the arrival of whatever it is they asked for. In the meantime, many seem to miss the God-given gifts which come their way. They fail to notice these blessings simply because they were not what they were expecting.

I have often said, "God works in strange ways." I'm absolutely convinced that God answers our prayers. I'm equally convinced, however, that the way God answers our prayers is not always what we had expected. For this reality, I'm incredibly grateful. Many of the gifts I've been given through the years were so much better than anything I had hoped for.

Trust me. It happens sometimes!

Reflection Questions:

1. Do you ask God for things? If so, after you've made your request, how do you cope with the waiting and anticipation of God's response?

2. Are you confident that God answers your prayers? If so, what gives you such confidence?

3. Have you ever, in retrospect, realized that what God provided for you was not only different, but, in fact, even better than what you had asked for?

7

Inappropriate Language

"Caution: Be sure brain is engaged
Before putting mouth in gear."
~ Author Unknown

I am not at all proud to share this story, but it's a lesson I learned which I felt compelled to share with every student I taught in my forty years in the classroom. Some important life lessons just have to be learned the hard way. Throughout my lifetime, there have been many things I've learned in ways I wish had been different. In the end, however, it has been some of these lessons which have had the most significant impact on my life.

During my sophomore year of high school, one of the seniors at my school invited me to join him for an after-school excursion. When I asked where we were going, he told me, "If I tell you, you won't want to go." Despite this ominous warning, I went with him. He was someone I trusted implicitly, so I knew there was nothing to fear. When we arrived at a house on Fulton Street between 2nd and 3rd Avenues, directly across the street from Golden Gate Park in San Francisco, I followed my friend up to the house. Instead of climbing the steps to the front door, he walked directly to the garage door and knocked. My suspicions were aroused. I was totally unprepared for what awaited me inside.

As we entered the garage, I found myself in an environment not unlike Santa's North Pole workshop. There were Christmas decorations throughout the room. And there, sitting around several tables, were mentally retarded adults, about a dozen in all, working diligently on various Christmas-themed arts and crafts projects. My friend introduced me to the director of Helpers Home for the Mentally Retarded. Then he introduced me to Tom, Jimmy, Sam, Frances, and Judy, some of the more socially-outgoing of the residents. From there, Judy took over as my guide and showed me around the workshop, explaining in detail the process of making assorted Christmas-themed items which would be sold at the Helpers Home Bazaar at Ghirardelli Square during the Christmas season. Judy also made it a point to proudly show me a photo of Rose Kennedy, mother of President John F. Kennedy, who had visited the facility several years before. Standing next to Mrs. Kennedy was a younger, and very proud, Judy.

For the next couple of years, I spent my after-school hours two or three days a week in the Fulton Street garage, working side-by-side with the residents doing whatever they were doing. One day I would be sewing eyes onto hand puppets with Tom, Jimmy and Sam. Another day I would be cracking walnuts with Frances, and sorting the edible parts from the shells. Over time, several of my classmates joined me in this after-school service opportunity. Girls from both Presentation High School and Star of the Sea Academy also volunteered there, which was definitely a perk for those of us who attended our all-boys high school.

One day, during my junior year, a group of us were sitting around a table in the Helpers Home garage — some guys from my school, a few girls, and a small group of Helpers Home residents. I don't recall exactly which project we had undertaken that day, but I vividly recall where I was sitting, and that my friend Bob was sitting directly across the table from me. I don't remember the topic of our conversation that afternoon, but I will never forget what I said when one of my high school classmates made a comment, most likely in jest, which I thought was ridiculous. My response was brief, and thoughtless: "You retard!"

Immediately the table went silent for what seemed to me to be an eternity. I realized right away what I had said and where I was. My eyes were riveted on whatever it was I was holding in my hands. I wanted to crawl under the table. In fact, I wanted to just crawl right out the door and never return. I was absolutely mortified at what I'd just said. Eventually, someone spoke up, but not in response to what I had said. Soon the conversation was lively again, as if I had never made the ignorant comment. I think I remained silent for the rest of the afternoon.

I did return to the Helper's Home many times after that day. No one ever said a word about my insensitive comment. After my high school graduation in June 1972, I moved to San José and my volunteer experience at the Helpers Home ended. My memory of that incredibly inappropriate comment has stayed with me to this day. Throughout my teaching career, whenever I heard a student, or one of my colleagues, use the word "retard" in a derogatory manner, I gave them a quick one-on-one lesson in appropriate social skills, sharing with them the valuable lesson I learned in high school.

It's time for us to remove the word "retard" from our inventory of derogatory comments.

Reflection Questions:

1. Have you ever said something inappropriate that, immediately after saying it, you realized should never have been said? How did you deal with this situation?

2. Are there other derogatory terms that you use which should be removed from your arsenal of verbal responses or comments?

3. Would you be comfortable calling someone — a family member, friend, neighbor, or coworker — to accountability for using such a demeaning, inappropriate term in a conversation with you?

8

The Challenge of Gratitude

"No matter our circumstances,
no matter our challenges or trials,
there is something in each day to embrace and cherish."
~ Dieter F. Uchtdorf

Since attending the weekend retreat at the Jesuit Retreat Center in Los Altos in November 2006, I have made a concerted effort to focus on gratitude. Sometimes such a focus can be incredibly difficult. My thoughts about what I'm grateful for can get clouded by the day-to-day stress of dealing with difficult people. I'll admit that my life was generally not overly-stressful, but every now and then, some random set of circumstances would come together like the ingredients of the perfect category five hurricane. Then... BAM! It would hit. Unlike a hurricane, however, which normally provides ample warning prior to its arrival, stress can hit almost instantaneously. We don't see it coming, then it blindsides us. Briefly dazed by the blow, we must make a heroic effort not to over-react, then decide how to effectively respond to the situation.

I used to react somewhat impulsively. Now, I wait. Well,... not exactly. When I'm upset, I find it helpful to write. In my younger years, I would spill my thoughts and emotions into a letter or e-mail and send it immediately. Over time, I realized that there are more effective ways of dealing with difficult people and stressful situations. Now, I still write. I just don't send it immediately. I click "Save Draft" instead, and allow myself to breathe for awhile. I still feel better, because I've written what I wanted to say, but by clicking "Save Draft," rather than "Send," I give myself time to pause, reflect, and, perhaps, become a bit more rational in my response. As a consequence, I've found that I don't always have the need to send what I've written. Just having written it often brings the needed relief.

Although it took many years to develop, I'm thankful for the gift of wisdom which has come with age and experience. Such wisdom has enabled me to respond more appropriately to the inevitable stresses which arise in my life, and to recognize the blessings of each day. I'm also thankful for people who are willing to work with me, talk with me, listen to me, and help me to resolve issues in respectful and mutually-beneficial ways.

Reflection Questions:

1. Have you ever made an effort to focus on gratitude for an extended period of time?

2. When the circumstances of your life come together like the ingredients of a perfect category five hurricane, how do you most often react/respond? Has this been effective for you?

3. What causes stress in your life? How might a focus on gratitude help you to cope more effectively with such stress?

9

Excess Baggage

"Everyone has baggage.
Maybe we should help each other carry it."
~ Rob Liano

$\mathcal{W}$e all carry it. Some of us more so than others. Maybe it's because we think we might need some of it again some day. Or, perhaps, we're just not ready to set it aside. Whatever the reason, most of us are, in some ways, bogged down with the burdensome weight of excess baggage. Those who travel on a regular basis learn the art of packing efficiently. Many business travelers rely solely on carry-on luggage. The rest of us, however, tend to carry with us much more than we're actually going to need — just in case. Life can be like this, too.

In my years of teaching, I often shared the image with my students of a "backpack of life" — an imaginary storage container we carry with us at all times. As we navigate the inevitable ups and downs of our existence, we can place the experiences and pearls of wisdom we acquire into our backpack. If something is not helpful to us, we can leave it where it is. Unfortunately, it's quite common for things to find their way into our backpack of life which don't necessarily serve us well in the long-run.

For example, many of us carry around an incredible amount of guilt, especially those of us raised in Catholic families, about our actions, or failures to act, or about choices we've made along the way. Or we may carry the burden of regret, often pertaining to opportunities we allowed to pass us by, or, perhaps, the way we treated someone at some point in our life journey. It's alarming how many of us drag anger around with us, for any number of reasons. In fact, it's not uncommon for one to hold onto anger toward those who may have hurt them as much as forty or fifty years ago. Trust me. I know.

A good number of us hold tight to resentment toward those who may have disappointed us at some point, or who failed in some way to meet our expectations. Feelings of inadequacy can weigh us down, too, often resulting from being unfairly compared with others — or from comparing ourselves with others. We can also carry the burden of shame, about our physical appearance or about some other aspect of ourselves, or embarrassment due to failures we may have experienced.

Fear and self-doubt can also be tremendous burdens we carry with us unnecessarily — fear about things which may never happen, or fear that others might find out that we're not who or what they thought we were — even if we are! And self-doubt can weigh us down when we truly believe that if others knew us as well as we know ourselves, they might not like or accept us.

As if that were not enough, another form of excess baggage might include envy toward those who have more than we do, or those who have achieved a greater level of success in life. Bitterness, too, can weigh us down, if we fail to let go of the painful memories of those who have used us or taken advantage of our kindness or generosity.

Now might be a good time for all of us to conduct an inventory of our backpack of life, hoping to let go of the excess baggage with which are we needlessly burdening ourselves. Perhaps, by doing so, we might make room for something a little more useful — like gratitude.

Reflection Questions:

1. What excess baggage do you carry with you at this point in your life? Where did you acquire it? Why do you continue to carry it around with you?

2. What specific strategies might you employ to help you let go of these things in your backpack of life which are weighing you down?

10

Mistakes

*"Mistakes are painful when they happen,
but years later, a collection of mistakes
is what is called experience."*
~ Denis Waitley

$\mathcal{A}$s I approach my mid-sixties, I have a great deal of experience. And yes, much of that experience is the result of a lifetime of mistakes. Some of those mistakes were obvious, some were avoidable, some were incredibly painful, and others just temporarily knocked me off-stride. All of these, however, contribute significantly to who I am today.

Given this understanding of experience, I guess what I'm really talking about here is wisdom.

I've never considered myself to be overly-intelligent. Yes, I have a Master's Degree, but that simply means I jumped through the hoops of academia for the prescribed number of years. I read the required texts, completed the required courses, participated in group discussions, and wrote more papers than I'd like to remember. While it was certainly a valuable learning experience, all I learned in the classroom pales in comparison to the lessons I've learned in life, quite often through my mistakes.

Throughout my life, I've acquired a fair amount of wisdom — information, insights, and experience, which has guided me through my adult life, and which, now and then, I have the opportunity to share with others. Through the years, I've shared much of this wisdom with my three boys in situations I like to call "teachable moments." In the classroom, I was able to share some of this wisdom with my students. On my *Attitude of Gratitude* blog site, I've shared much of what I've learned in life with those who happen to read my posts. And in casual conversations with friends, I often have the opportunity to share little tidbits of my lived experience, as I listen and learn from the little tidbits of their lived experience. I've even taken the opportunity to share some of what I've learned in life with my friends on Facebook.

When I was younger, I was very impressed with information, and I tried to impress others by displaying evidence of the information I had absorbed in my academic studies. Now I realize the shortcomings of information alone. Our society today is inundated with information. The technology available to us in this still-new millennium bombards us with more information than we can possibly handle. There seems to be, however, a shortage of wisdom in the world today, and those who possess wisdom, and dare to share it with others, are often perceived as outdated, obsolete, or no longer relevant because the wisdom they share doesn't seem quite as practical as the current information streaming through our latest tech devices.

I'm tremendously grateful for what I learned in school. Much of that information has helped me to be a productive member of society. I'm even more grateful, however, for the wisdom I've acquired through the years, and for the wisdom I have yet to acquire. I've come to appreciate that, while information can help us to live a successful life, it is wisdom which enables us to live life to the fullest.

Reflection Questions:

1. Do you tend to place a greater value on *information* or on *wisdom*? Why?

2. When you think of all the wisdom you've acquired in your lifetime, is there one particular lesson you learned which you would like to share with the next generation?

11

Living Simply

"Our life is frittered away by detail.
Simplify. Simplify."
~ Henry David Thoreau

*H*ow can we live a simple lifestyle when we have so much?

I remember back in the early 1980's when, after graduating from Santa Clara University, I lived in a modest two-bedroom rental home on Lincoln Street in Santa Clara, California. I didn't have much, but I had all I needed. Most of what I owned was second-hand stuff. The furniture in every room had been given to me by an assortment of friends and family members. A redwood picnic table in the back yard had been hand-made by one of my high school buddies. Even the two captain's chairs which sat on my front porch had been left there by previous renters. Life was simple then, and it was good... very good!

Life is good now, too, but over the past thirty-two years, my wife and I have accumulated an incredible amount of "stuff." Much of it is very nice. It's just that we have so much more than we need. So how can we live a life of simplicity when our home is filled with so many things that really aren't necessary for our survival?

I guess the real question is: "What, exactly, is a life of simplicity?" Maybe living a life of simplicity is more than just doing without today's most coveted consumer items. Maybe it's an attitude — an attitude of gratitude for all the possessions we own. Maybe it's more of an Ignatian-style detachment from those material possessions. Or, perhaps, it's a challenge to find ways to use the things we have *"for the greater glory of God."*

I'm immensely grateful for what we have, even though I would happily rent a U-Haul truck tomorrow and bring much of it to the San José Family Shelter to be given to families who need these items more than we do. I could probably fill a truck to capacity with items we would never miss. And think of all the extra room we'd have in our home and garage!!!

Throughout my life, I've made a concerted effort to live a life of simplicity. This is something I intend to continue. Yes, there are items we need and there are things we want, but maintaining an attitude of detachment can allow us to avoid letting our possessions possess us. It might also be a good idea for me to keep a Post-It with the phone number for U-Haul near the phone.

Reflection Questions:

1. Do you have a desire to live a more simple lifestyle than the one you're living now? Why, or why not?

2. What, if anything, prevents you from detaching from some of your possessions?

3. Have you considered the possibility that some of your possessions — things you rarely, if ever use — might be put to immediate use by someone who struggles to acquire life's most basic necessities?

12

Why Work So Hard?

"With slight efforts,
how can we obtain great results?
It is foolish even to desire it."
~ Euripides

In his best-selling book, <u>Summer of '49</u>, baseball enthusiast and award-winning author David Halberstam wrote of a question posed to baseball legend Joe DiMaggio late in his stellar career with the New York Yankees. He was enduring constant pain in his legs and feet at that time. The Yankees enjoyed a comfortable late-season lead in the pennant race. It was then that columnist Jimmy Cannon asked DiMaggio why he played so hard when the games, at that point in the season, didn't mean so much? DiMaggio responded, "Because there might be somebody out there who's never seen me play before."

When I read that sentence, I put a bookmark in the page and closed the book. It wasn't the last chapter. In fact, it wasn't even the end of a chapter. DiMaggio's response was just one of those statements that I needed some time to digest. It was, for me, one of those ah-ha moments.

I doubt that I have much in common with Joe DiMaggio. During his years with the Yankees, he was one of those larger-than-life celebrities.

I'm not. While I have always liked the game of baseball, it was not a sport in which I excelled. Like DiMaggio, however, I was a professional. I took great pride in what I did as an educator, and I cared about how I was perceived by my students, their parents, my colleagues, and school administrators.

When my teaching career, to put it into into baseball terms, got into the late innings, some people asked me why I put so much time and effort into preparing my classes each week. This is where DiMaggio's response to Jimmy Cannon's question struck a chord with me. I might have been near the end of my teaching career, but just as each day in a major league baseball stadium brings in a new crowd, in each year of teaching, I was greeted by a new group of students, students who had never experienced me as their teacher. Like DiMaggio, I wanted them to see me at my best.

When I picked up Halberstam's <u>Summer of '49</u>, I thought I was doing so to escape reality for awhile, to get away from thoughts about school and teaching, and to immerse myself in a major league pennant race which took place five years before I was born. I had not expected to be jolted out of my comfort zone by such an insightful comment by a highly-respected professional athlete.

I am always grateful for pearls of wisdom, wherever I find them. I will always be grateful for the wealth of knowledge and wisdom I've learned through my participation in organized sports, through meeting coaches and athletes who were willing to share their wisdom, and from books and movies which use sports to help us make sense of this game we call life. I can use all the help I can get!

Reflection Questions:

1. What significant lesson(s), if any, have you learned from sports?

2. Many coaches and players from various sports have written books about their experiences. Is there any one coach or athlete whose book inspired you or provided wisdom from which you have benefitted in your lifetime?

13

A Time to Surrender

*"Life is a balance between
what we can control and what we cannot.
I am learning to live between
effort and surrender."*
~ Danielle Orner

We've seen it in the old war movies — the white flag waving in defeat as the combatants walk out into the open with their hands in the air, having lost the hard-fought battle or, perhaps, having chosen not to fight at all. Most of us learn the term "surrender" at an early age. Unfortunately, we learn only one understanding of the word — to cut our losses and give up to the more dominant power. So why, then, throughout so much of my life, have I been able to experience such a tremendous sense of peace by surrendering to the way things were in my life? Did I give up? Did I lack initiative? Was I defeated by a more powerful force? I certainly don't see it that way.

The word "surrender" can be understood in a very different way, as freely giving over or resigning oneself to a particular situation. There is a huge difference between *giving up* and *giving over*. I've never thought of myself as a quitter, and on more than one occasion I've dug my heels in to stand up for what I believed to be right, even when my opinion was at odds with those around me. But as the *Book of Ecclesiastes* says so eloquently, there is a time for everything. Yes, even surrender.

This is certainly not a well-kept secret, it's just something that many of us have chosen to ignore. The Islam faith is based on the concept of surrender. In Christianity, the virtue of surrender can be found in many places, including the spirituality of Saint Ignatius of Loyola:

> *"Take, Lord, and receive all my liberty,*
> *my memory, understanding, and my entire will,*
> *all I have and call my own.*
> *You have given all to me. To you, Lord, I return it.*
> *Everything is yours; do with it what you will.*
> *Give me only your love and your grace.*
> *That is enough for me."*

To surrender does not necessarily mean to lose or to be defeated. It can also be understood as letting go or turning things over to God.

In the past several years, I have given considerable thought to this concept. I made a conscientious effort to listen, to allow God to guide me regarding how to handle some challenging situations and a few difficult people. Throughout my life, I've always been quite self-sufficient, able to handle just about any situation on my own. Yet the most positive, life-changing experiences in my life have resulted not from my own initiative, but from those times when I let go and allowed God to lead me. My experiences working in Jamaica and the Bahamas, my various teaching jobs, and even the opportunities I had to visit Japan, all resulted from saying "Yes" to opportunities which were unexpectedly presented to me, not through anything I actively initiated.

I am grateful to have learned that to surrender is neither an act of weakness nor desperation. Rather, it is an act of faith.

Reflection Questions:

1. Have you ever found yourself involved in a situation in which you realized that you were not going to achieve your intended goal?

2. In that situation, were you able to surrender — to put it in God's hands and trust that, in the end, things would work out for the best?

14

Life Isn't Fair

"The rain falls on the just and the unjust alike."
~ Charles Schulz

Rabbi Harold Kushner, after the premature death of his fourteen-year-old son, set out to write a book about his experience of grief. He wanted to write about why bad things happen to good people. It didn't take him long to realize that there is no answer to this question. So he changed the title of his book to <u>When Bad Things Happen to Good People</u>. It became a *New York Times* best-seller, much to his surprise and that of the publishing companies which initially rejected his manuscript.

Yes, unfortunate occurrences happen all to often, and they seem to be an equal-opportunity experience. I see homeless men and women throughout the Santa Clara Valley and ask myself why they are in that position. I heard about the student-athlete at a local high school who took a clean hit in a football game on Thanksgiving Day a few years ago and ended up in a coma. I couldn't help but think that could have been one of my kids. And I recently heard about a family in Northern California who lost their home in a fire a week before Christmas. The parents and their nine children ended up living in a studio apartment until they could get their lives back together. Why do these things have to happen? Why do bad things have to happen to anyone?

I don't know. It's really that simple. I just don't know. Rabbi Kushner came to the same conclusion. So dwelling on this question might be an exercise in futility. Perhaps a better question to be asking is "What now?"

In the case of homeless people, the "what now?" might be for us to assist them in finding appropriate support from agencies geared to serving those in similar situations. In regards to the high school football player, friends and extended family might consider providing the player's family with meals, help with yard work, or simply offering the gift of their presence. For the family whose home burned to the ground, the "what now?" might include supporting the family with food, clothing, household items, babysitting, or, perhaps, even a spare room in one's home. Of course, for all of them, the "what now?" might also include a healthy dose of prayer.

One of the greatest mistakes a person can make life is to think that life is fair. It isn't. The reality of life is that sometimes bad things are going to happen to those perceived as good, and sometimes those perceived as not-so-good may come out smelling like a rose. We don't think it's supposed to happen this way, but sometimes it does.

As long as we don't expect life to be fair, we are less likely to be disappointed. At the same time, we have to be careful not to become cynical or pessimistic. Life may not be fair, but it is usually very good if we allow it to be! For this I am exceedingly grateful.

Reflection Questions:

1. Have you been confronted with the reality of something bad happening to someone you consider to be a good person — someone you think should not have had to deal with that particular negative experience? How did you deal with this situation?

2. Is it possible to acknowledge that life is not fair, yet still maintain a positive outlook on life, as well as a true sense of gratitude?

3. What role does prayer play in your life as you struggle to cope with difficult, even painful experiences?

15

On Doing Nothing

"Never be afraid to sit awhile and think."
~ Lorainne Hansberry

In a world where we are frequently judged by our level of productivity, sitting around "doing nothing" is often frowned upon. It seems that we are expected to produce evidence to justify how we've spent our time. For this reason, I am grateful for the soothing words of Lorainne Hansberry, author of <u>A Raisin in the Sun</u>, in the quote above.

When it comes right down to it, it is virtually impossible for us to do nothing. No matter what we're doing or not doing, we're always doing something. We might be sitting in a comfortable chair reminiscing about our childhood. We might be looking out the living room window wishing the weather was a bit warmer or cooler. We might be sitting in front of the television watching reruns of *The Andy Griffith Show*, *My Three Sons*, or *Hogan's Heroes*. When others may perceive that we are doing nothing, in reality, we are always doing something.

I received an interesting email from a friend recently. She asked me a rather strange question: Do I read during the day? And, if so, do I feel guilty doing so? She went on to explain that, in her childhood, she got the message that "doing nothing" was unacceptable — sinful, in fact

— and that reading during the day was tantamount to doing nothing. Yes, she's Irish-Catholic, and that Irish-Catholic guilt consumed her at an early age, perhaps due to the fact that her father had expressed the same sentiment regarding daytime reading.

In my response to her email, I reminded my friend that some of the lessons we learned in our youth don't necessarily serve us so well as we get older. I assured her that, yes, I read during the day — quite regularly, in fact. Reading, or the ability to read, is a God-given gift. So, too, is our desire to read. Mark Twain once said that those who do not read have no advantage over those who cannot read. Reading most certainly is "doing something." It's using our God-given gift to relax, to entertain, to learn, to inspire,... These are all good things.

I confidently assured my friend that there is absolutely nothing wrong with reading during the day. In fact, what might be wrong, if anything, would be to NOT read when we have the ability to do so. By reading, we are utilizing that God-given gift, and we are all called to put our God-given gifts to good use. I'm tremendously grateful for the gift of reading — and for the desire to do so.

Reflection Questions:

1. Have you ever had to defend something you were doing which someone else thought was simply a waste of time?

2. What lessons did you learn in your younger years which, upon further review, were proven to be less than helpful in your adult life?

3. Have you ever considered the wisdom contained in Mark Twain's quote that those who do not read have no advantage over those who cannot read?

16

Learning to Say "No"

*"It's only by saying 'No' that you can
concentrate on the things that are really important."*
~ Steve Jobs

*N*ancy Reagan made it sound so easy. *"Just Say No!"* It's as simple as that, right? Well,... not exactly. Saying "No" is a difficult thing to do, especially when you've been taught in catholic schools to be a "good little boy" and to be cooperative whenever people ask for your help.

I've spent most of my life saying "Yes," even when I've wanted to say "No." I've committed myself to meetings, dinner engagements, coaching jobs, committees, purchases, workshops, dates, and a number of other activities when I wanted to say "No" and should have said "No!" For me, and for many others, however, saying "No" just wasn't that easy. It has taken me a long time, but little by little, I've learned to do just that.

The first time I consciously asserted my right to say "No," despite the awkwardness I felt in doing so, was about a dozen years ago. I was in a meeting at the high school where I was a teacher. We were in the early stages of our school's accreditation process. Each member of the faculty and staff had been assigned to a small group. The first task for each group was to identify someone to lead the group. One member of the group to which I had been assigned, without hesitation, volunteered me for the leadership role. Maybe I should have considered it a compliment, but I didn't. I was offended by the way it was done. I didn't appreciate someone, who would never have volunteered for the leadership role herself, just throwing my name out for consideration. For perhaps the first time in my life, I said firmly, "I can't do it." There was absolute silence in the room. *Did he say,... "No"?* Once the initial shock of my unexpected response wore off, two other group members volunteered to co-chair the group. They did a great job. Saying "No" felt absolutely wonderful!

I wish I could say that I learned my lesson that day. I didn't. Since then, I've continued to say "Yes" when I really wanted to say "No," but I've learned that it's okay to change my mind, too. On a number of occasions recently, I've contacted the person to whom I had hastily made a commitment and apologetically retracted that commitment. Hopefully some day soon, I'll learn to defer responding immediately and to give myself some time to discern whether or not I am able and willing to make the commitment. That will definitely be a step in the right direction.

I'm grateful to have learned this important life lesson, difficult as it has been to learn. I am still willing to help others and to be a team player when I feel that it is the right thing to do, but I've learned that saying "No" is an acceptable, and sometimes necessary option.

Reflection Questions:

1. Do you have the ability to say "No" when you're asked to do something you'd rather not do?

2. Can you recall a time when you regretted committing yourself to something too hastily?

3. Do you agree that backing out of a hastily-made commitment is an acceptable, understandable, and sometimes necessary strategy for self-care?

17

Learning from Social Cruelty

"And once the storm is over,
you won't remember how you made it through.
You won't be the same person who walked in.
That's what this storm's all about."
~ Haruki Murakami

It all began with a joke. An Italian joke. I didn't think it was offensive or in any way disrespectful. It certainly wasn't meant to be. I thought it was clever and funny, so I shared it with one of my sixth grade classmates, who was Italian-American. He thought it was pretty funny, too. A day or so later, he shared it with some of our other classmates at school, several of whom also happened to be of Italian descent, giving me credit for the humor. Some of them, apparently, didn't think the joke was funny at all — especially coming from someone with Irish-American roots.

The next two and a half years of my life gave me a glimpse of what Hell must be like. I immediately became a social outcast. No longer was I one of the normal kids in my class. No longer was I chosen to play in the lunchtime kickball games. No longer was I welcome to sit with my classmates while we ate our lunches. And, if that wasn't harsh enough, I endured more than two years of physical, emotional, and verbal abuse by a relatively small group of self-proclaimed "popular" classmates who seemed to take great satisfaction in tormenting me and some of my classmates.

It might sound strange, but that experience, perhaps more than any other in my lifetime, made me a better teacher. Had I not experienced that exclusion by my classmates during my middle school years, I may not have had the perspective, the compassion, nor the empathy for the social outcasts I encountered during my years as a middle school and high school teacher.

Social cruelty in schools is an epidemic. It was a problem in 1966 and it continues to be a problem today. It doesn't happen only in public schools. Social cruelty is just as much of a reality in catholic and private schools. Unfortunately, until recently, it was not high on the list of critical issues in education. It is now.

I spent a considerable amount of time discussing social cruelty with my students through the years. I identified the problem, and shared with them the hierarchy, or social class structure, which exists among students in just about every school. My students readily acknowledged the validity of my observations and agreed that those observations accurately described their particular group of students. The primary difference between my middle school experience of exclusion and the social cruelty kids endure today is the bully's use of social media. Now, instead of being harassed only while on campus, victims can be bullied online day and night.

My middle school years were a painful time, but I'm honestly grateful for what I learned from the social cruelty. Because of those experiences, I was a better teacher, and I think a better person, than I might otherwise have been.

Reflection Questions:

1. Were you ever the victim (or perpetrator) of social cruelty? What did you learn from the experience?

2. Did you experience other hardships in your life which, despite the pain they may have caused you, were learning experiences which made you a better person?

3. Have you observed or experienced social cruelty in the workplace? What, if anything, can be done to deal effectively with workplace bullying?

18

What's In Your Wallet?

"The most fundamental attack on freedom
is the attack on critical thinking skills."
~ Travis Nichols

"On sale! Don't miss this offer! For a limited time only! Call now! Don't be left out! For ONLY thirty-six payments of $24.95 — Yes, ONLY $24.95..." Hey, wait a minute! That's almost $900!!! (*"Yes,... but we don't want to talk about that right now, do we?"*)

"You can afford it! You deserve it! Don't embarrass your wife and children by allowing your neighbor to show you up again! It's all about the competition! He who dies with the most toys wins, right?"

Advertising today is relentless. Using a variety of tactics, which industry experts must validate as being effective, advertisers seek to create in consumers a void, a sense that they are somehow deprived, yet deserving of whatever product is being promoted — whether they can actually afford it or not. Creating a sense of urgency (*"Don't wait!"*) and entitlement (*"You deserve this..."*), they tap into the consumer's emotional need for approval, acceptance, and recognition. Both men and women are targets of such manipulative advertising.

The bottom line is that the media is selling us on a lifestyle which, in reality, is unattainable for most of us. Since when is a $60,000 car "affordable"? There are a few strategies which can help a consumer to minimize the effects of such shrewd advertising tactics. Three tools come to mind: (1) critical thinking skills, (2) self-discipline, and (3) common sense.

The website of *The Critical Thinking Community* defines critical thinking as *"…that mode of thinking — about any subject, content, or problem — in which the thinker improves the quality of his or her thinking by skillfully analyzing, assessing, and reconstructing it. Critical thinking is self-directed, self-disciplined, self-monitored, and self-corrective thinking."* This is a learned skill. Only in recent years have most schools made a conscientious effort to teach such skills.

When I speak of self-discipline, I am referring to the one question a consumer should ask him/herself prior to committing to any significant purchase: "Do I want it or do I need it?" This relatively simple question can save consumers an incredible amount of money, heartache, and regret throughout their lifetime.

Common sense, too, is essential if we wish to avoid falling prey to shrewd advertising. Unfortunately, common sense is not so common in the world today. Common sense would urge us to ask: "Can I afford this?" Not everyone would agree with my definition of "afford." Credit cards often give consumers the mistaken belief that they can afford a product. Yes, a credit card may enable one to leave the store with the product in hand, but does that consumer have the cash on hand to pay that credit card bill — in full — when it arrives? If the answer is "No," then, generally speaking, they cannot afford the item.

I'm grateful to have learned critical thinking skills in high school and college. Such skills have been a part of Jesuit education for generations. I'm grateful to my parents for instilling in me the self-discipline I need to keep myself out of financial distress. It's a lesson I learned early in life. And I'm grateful for the gift of common sense. While I have not always shown evidence of such a gift in my lifetime, I'm confident that it is something which has served me well through the years.

Reflection Questions:

1. Have you ever fallen prey to manipulative advertising? Have you made a purchase which, upon further review, was ill-advised?

2. Are you in the habit of asking the "want vs. need" question when considering a significant purchase? How might asking this question affect your purchasing patterns?

3. What strategies do you employ to help you make good purchasing choices and avoid the pressure of today's devious advertising ploys?

19

Responsible Parenting

*"Life affords no greater responsibility,
no greater privilege,
than the raising of the next generation."*
~ C. Everett Koop

*P*arenting isn't easy. Some people, it seems, just don't accept the challenge, choosing instead to be more concerned with being their child's friend than embracing the role of parent. It's sad, because young people today don't need forty- or fifty-year old friends. They need parents — real parents — who take their responsibility seriously.

In my thirty-plus years as a parent, I've seen and heard many incredible stories of parents not doing their job. In some cases, they turn a blind eye to their teen's drinking or drug use. In other cases, parents, by their own example, teach their children to cheat and lie. Neale Donald Walsch, author of <u>Conversations with God</u>, reminds us of one of the most challenging aspects of parenting. He wrote, *"Teach not with your words, but with your actions; not with discussion, but with demonstration. For it is what you do that your children will emulate, and how you are that they will become."*

Despite all the bad news about irresponsible parenting, some parents are doing an amazing job of raising their children. I witnessed such a situation one evening when my youngest son, Brendan, was a freshman in high school. He had been invited to a "Sweet Sixteen" birthday party for a girl from his school who was a year older. My wife and I drove Brendan to the family's home. We had been invited to stop by briefly, as the birthday girl was one of my students. We accompanied Brendan to the front door, much to his embarrassment, I'm sure. Standing at the front door were two adult men — the birthday girl's uncle and a neighbor, who happened to be a retired San José police officer. With guest list in hand, they warmly welcomed each student and discretely observed them for evidence of use or possession of alcohol or drugs.

In conversation with the parents, I learned that every bottle of alcohol normally kept in the kitchen in their home had been moved to the next-door neighbor's home for the evening. All bedroom doors were locked. There were enough adults present — parents, neighbors, aunts, and uncles — to have adequate adult supervision in the front room, kitchen, and back yard. And all attendees had been notified on the party invitation that they would not be allowed to leave the party and return.

Despite what might have otherwise seemed like an oppressive environment, the party atmosphere was festive. The kids had a great time. There was good music, alternative lighting, and an abundance of good food and beverages.

It was so refreshing to see parents take their role as parents seriously. They were able to provide an enjoyable, yet safe environment for their daughter's sixteenth birthday party. As a parent, I was tremendously grateful for their effort. I think the kids were, too.

Reflection Questions:

1. In what other ways is it possible for parents to "be parents" to their children? Is it wrong for parents to want to be friends with their kids?

2. Can you recall an experience in which you were totally impressed with someone's parenting skills? What was it about this person which made such a positive impression on you?

3. If you are a parent, what one parenting tip would you share with young parents today?

20

A Year to Remember

"Say 'Yes,' and you'll figure it out afterwards."
~ Tina Fey

I was only twenty years old when I began teaching Religious Studies at Saint Augustine's College in the Bahamas in 1974. Despite my age and lack of credentials, I took off from San Francisco International Airport in late August for what was, perhaps, the most significant experience of my life.

Three years earlier, in the summer of 1971, I had spent six weeks working in Jamaica with one of my high school teachers and Dan Pasini, one of my classmates at Saint Ignatius College Prep. During our time there, we were invited to join the Jesuit community at Campion College in Kingston for a celebration of the Feast of Saint Ignatius of Loyola on July 31st. It was there that we met Father Elias Achatz, O.S.B., a Benedictine monk who lived and worked in Nassau. In the spring of 1974, Father Elias contacted my classmate and me to inquire as to our availability to spend a year in Nassau, teaching Religious Studies at Saint Augustine's. We both accepted the offer.

Father Elias was the prior of the Benedictine community in the monastery and the head of the Religious Studies Department at the school. He met Dan and me at the airport in Nassau. We took the scenic route to "SAC," where we would live in guest rooms adjacent to the monastery for the next year. We got right down to work the following day with an orientation for the new expatriate teachers. Before I knew it, there I was standing in front of a class of Bahamian high school students, several of whom were about my age.

In some ways, I was very comfortable in my new job. I had taught a sixth grade religious education class at Our Lady of Mercy School in Daly City, California during my senior year of high school. I had also spent two years working as a prefect in the student dormitory at Bellarmine College Preparatory in San José. These experiences gave me the confidence to take on the responsibilities of teaching in the highly-respected island high school. It was definitely a learning experience. Day by day, I gained both confidence and competence in my new role.

It was a life-changing adventure for me. Prior to my arrival in Nassau, I didn't have a clear sense of direction in my life. I had contemplated a career in firefighting, and, even while in Nassau, continued to wrestle with the possibility of a vocation to the Jesuit priesthood. That one year at Saint Augustine's, however, gave me the sense of direction and purpose I needed. After a brief six-month stint at the Jesuit Novitiate in Montecito, California, a wonderful experience which I will never regret, I enrolled at Santa Clara University, where I had all the motivation I needed to meet the academic challenges of the curriculum. I knew I wanted to teach, and I knew what I had to do to achieve that goal.

It seems like an understatement to say that I'm grateful for my unique Bahamian experience. Of course I am! To this day, I am convinced that God had plans for me which I did not have for myself. The unexpected invitation to teach at SAC enabled me to learn, with a sense of certainty, that I was meant to teach. I'm grateful that now, in my retirement, I can look back on my forty years of teaching with a sense of accomplishment and fulfillment.

Reflection Questions:

1. Can you recall any unique experiences which presented you with an opportunity to better understand your purpose in life?

2. Have you had an experience in your life which you would describe as "life-changing"?

3. Have you ever accepted a job or taken on a responsibility for which you were unqualified? If so, what was the outcome of this experience?

21

Play Ball!

"Love is the most important thing in the world,
but baseball is pretty good, too."
~ Yogi Berra

April is a great month. It's spring. Therefore, it's baseball season! All three of my boys played Little League ball. Steve and Brendan both played varsity baseball in high school. Steve went on to play in college, too. The beginning of every season always holds such promise. Whether watching my kids play or following the San Francisco Giants, I'm always grateful for the start of a new season.

For most Americans, baseball is more than simply a game. It's an institution. It doesn't matter if the game is being played at Wrigley Field in Chicago, Yankee Stadium in the Bronx, Fenway Park in Boston, or AT&T Park on the edge of San Francisco Bay. Baseball is baseball, complete with all its history and memories.

I remember my first Giants' game in August of 1964. Actually, I remember the day before my first Giants' game. I got two free tickets for delivering the *Shopping News* in the City that summer. My neighbor had the route, but he went out of town for the summer months, so I took over the route for him. One of the perks of delivering the paper twice each week was receiving a set of tickets to a game between the San Francisco Giants and the Cincinnati Reds at Candlestick Park.

The day of the game, I was planning to take the San Francisco Muni "Ballpark Express" to the game with my friend, so my Dad took me out to the ballpark the day before to show me around. We didn't need tickets to get into the stadium that day. Dad simply flashed his San Francisco Fire Department badge and explained the situation to the gatekeeper. We entered the huge concrete structure and walked up the ramp to the upper deck.

My first view of the playing field was breathtaking. As we walked through the tunnel into the seating area, the drab grey of the stadium was replaced by the dazzling emerald green of the outfield grass. I couldn't believe my eyes. I just stood there in amazement and took it all in.

Immediately, Dad started pointing out the players -- Harvey Kuenn, Willie Mays, and Willie McCovey patrolled the outfield. Orlando Cepeda, Hal Lanier, José Pagan, and Jim Davenport handled the infield duties. Tom Haller was behind the plate, with Ron Herbel on the mound. I was absolutely in awe.

I have to admit that I still experience that same sense of awe when I walk into the Giants' ballpark today. AT&T is spectacular, compared to the drab gray of Candlestick Park. In addition to the green grass, the stadium offers amazing views of San Francisco Bay and the now famous "McCovey Cove." The signature *Coca Cola* bottle behind the left field bleachers leaves no doubt about where the game is being played. AT&T Park is an iconic venue for baseball. Other than Candlestick and the Oakland Colosseum, I don't have anything to compare it to, but I can't imagine a better environment for a game of baseball.

I'm grateful for the opportunity to get to a few Giants' games each year. It's a bit of an adventure taking the train from the South Bay, but the experience of seeing a live professional baseball game in a stadium as beautiful as AT&T Park is something I'll never take for granted.

Reflection Questions:

1. What is your favorite professional baseball team? What is your favorite professional baseball stadium?

2. What recollections do you have of your first professional sporting event? If sports isn't your thing, is there a concert or theater production you attended which brings back special memories?

22

38th Avenue

*"One day, if I go to Heaven, I'll look around and say,
'It ain't bad, but it ain't San Francisco.'"*
~ Herb Caen

I was born and raised in San Francisco. Having lived there for the first eighteen years of my life, I got to know The City fairly well. Even now, after living most of my adult life in the Santa Clara Valley, about fifty miles south of The City, I still enjoy giving tours of San Francisco to out-of-town guests. It's not unusual for people to call me and ask for directions to get where they want to go in San Francisco.

There's one street that I know better than the rest — 38th Avenue, between Vicente and Wawona Streets, in the Sunset District. This was the street of my childhood. This is where I learned to ride a bike and how to roller skate. This is where we tossed baseballs, footballs, frisbees, and just about anything else that could be tossed. The neighborhood kids would play hide and seek, kick-the-can, and kickball on 38th Avenue. We'd set off fireworks on the Fourth of July, back in the day when fireworks were legal in San Francisco. And my first paid job was cutting the lawns of several houses on this street. This was my turf.

I still try to visit San Francisco on a fairly regular basis and, when I do, I almost always take a few minutes to either drive or walk down 38th Avenue. When I do this, I can't help but recall the countless trips I made up and down this street while on my way to South Sunset Playground, Saint Gabriel School, Fairlane Foods, and, during my high school years, to Saint Ignatius College Preparatory. The sidewalks of 38th Avenue were well worn by my travels.

For several years in my childhood, my paternal grandmother lived in the corner house at 38th & Vicente. I often stopped by to see her on my way home from classes at Saint Gabriel. I have fond memories of drinking Coca Cola in glass bottles, enjoying Coke floats at her kitchen table, and joining her for the latest installment of *The Merv Griffin Show* on TV in the afternoon.

38th Avenue is very different today. I grew up at a time when we knew all of our neighbors by name, when everyone on the block, or just about everyone, spoke the same language, and when the smell of freshly-fried fish permeated the neighborhood on Friday evenings. In my childhood, it was not uncommon for a neighbor to ring our doorbell and ask to borrow a cup of flour or sugar, or perhaps a couple of eggs. For the most part, everyone in the neighborhood watched out for and took care of everyone else. 38th Avenue was definitely a community.

I'm very grateful for the years I lived in The City. I'm grateful for people like Lloyd and Lillian Gray, who lived next door, and Bill and Elaine Cilia, who lived directly across the street from our home. If I ever got locked out of the house, I knew I could get a key from them. In many ways, they were like additional sets of parents. They cared about us and took an interest in our well-being. I'm grateful for Viola Frustruck, the elderly woman who lived two houses up the street. I could always count on her to purchase Christmas holly, raffle tickets, or whatever else I was asked to sell for the Scouts or for my schools. To express her appreciation for the "opportunity" to purchase these valuable items, she would offer me home-baked cookies. Such a deal!

I experienced a strong sense of belonging on 38th Avenue. For this, I will be forever grateful.

Reflection Questions:

1. What memories do you have of the neighborhood in which you grew up?

2. For what, or whom, in your childhood neighborhood are you most grateful?

3. If you could make one change to the neighborhood in which you currently reside, what might that change be?

23

Wisdom from Other Cultures

*"A single arrow is easily broken,
but not ten in a bundle."*
~ Japanese Proverb

There is so much we can learn from other cultures. For example, in the Chinese language, the word "crisis," as we understand it in English, is represented by two characters. Together the two characters mean *crisis*, as we understand it. Independently, however, each has its own meaning: one means *danger*, the other means *opportunity*. Knowing this invites and challenges us to look at any crisis situation with both caution and hope. What is the danger? What is the opportunity?

The Japanese language, too, has an important lesson for us. In that language, the English word "busy" can be understood to mean "to lose one's mind." I guess there's wisdom in that, too. It seems that many people experience this very feeling when they find themselves overwhelmed with the challenges of day-to-day living. That's why it's so important for us to have balance in our lives. I like to work hard, but not too hard. I like to eat, but not too much. I like to sleep, but not too much. Balance in life is essential to good health — both physical and mental health.

I recently came across a Turkish proverb which rings true in my experience: *"Who has never been burned in the sun won't know the value of shadow."* This is practical wisdom for someone, like me, who failed to adequately protect his skin in his younger years. I am now dealing with the unfortunate consequences of such negligence. The quote, however, also reminds me that only after being a well-known public figure can one truly appreciate the gift of anonymity.

I learned about the Chinese understanding of crisis in a book I read many years ago — Men in Midlife Crisis, by Jim Conway. I actually purchased and read the book, though I'm not exactly sure what prompted me to do so. I was only in my mid-thirties at the time. It was a good read.

I learned about the Japanese understanding of "busy" from my good friend Yuichiro Wakiyama, a teacher of English, who lives and works in Nagasaki, Japan. He shared this wisdom with me in a recent e-mail. It reminded me how important it is to maintain balance in one's life.

There is much to learn from our neighbors in other countries, wisdom that can help us to live life fully, the way our lives were meant to be lived. I'm grateful for such wisdom, and for the opportunity to incorporate it into my own life.

Reflection Questions:

1. Have you ever considered the optimistic outlook of the Chinese understanding of the word "crisis"? Are you able to recognize the opportunity which might exist in any difficult situation?

2. How do you cope with the busyness of your own life? How might you integrate a better sense of balance into your day-to-day activities?

3. Have you ever had the experience of being so well-known in a particular setting that you were recognize just about everywhere you went?

24

Simple Gratitude

"A poem begins in delight and ends in wisdom."
~ Robert Frost

We take so much for granted,
though our lives are truly blessed.
Are all of us entitled,
or is life a daily test?
Our days are filled with choices,
we can choose our attitude,
so why not try to focus more
on simple gratitude?

Just think about the gifts we have,
our sight, our home, our health;
we may not have much money,
but our life is filled with wealth.
The gift of education,
our family, friends, and food.
Why don't we focus more each day
on simple gratitude?

And think of opportunities
we've had throughout our days.
No doubt, we truly have been blessed
in countless other ways.
When people do nice things for us
to help improve our mood,
how much they would appreciate
our simple gratitude.

Each day that we awaken
there are choices we can make,
but thinking only of ourselves
would be a big mistake.
When people brighten up our day
it's best we not be rude.
A good response for all of us
is simple gratitude.

And even when life's challenges
bring obstacles and pain,
we have the choice to maintain hope
despite the clouds or rain.
We have this option every day:
to choose our attitude.
It just makes sense that we would choose
to live with gratitude.

So as you go about your life
consider all the ways
that you've been blessed with so much love
to brighten up your days.
For those who want a better life,
contented and renewed,
it's best that we devote ourselves
to simple gratitude!

Reflection Questions:

1. Do you find yourself feeling entitled, in any way, for the blessings you've received in your life — or can you say with certainty that you are truly grateful for these gifts, acknowledging that many of them are, in reality, absolutely undeserved?

2. Do you agree that living life with an attitude of gratitude is a choice? If so, how might consciously doing so affect your life?

25

The Gift of Typing

*"There is always, always, always
something to be thankful for."*
~ Author Unknown

$\mathcal{A}$SDF JKL; ASDF JKL; ASDF JKL; asdf jkl; asdf jkl; asdf jkl; That's how it all began in Mr. McDonald's first-semester Typing class at S.I. in September 1968. Practice and repetition — lots of practice and repetition. Little did I know that I would look back at this experience as one of the most valuable courses I took in my four years of high school.

I type every day. Whether I was preparing lesson plans during my teaching career, corresponding by e-mail, or updating my blog site, I use the skills I first learned in my freshman-year Typing class every day. Like most students, I didn't think the class was very important at the time. If it was really all that important, why did they have the varsity football coach teaching the class? Was he an expert at typing or did he simply need something to do during the day to keep him occupied until practice began at 3:15? I don't know.

How many of my high school classes directly impact my life today? Not many. I certainly don't have much need today for Chemistry, Algebra, or Physics. It's been a long time since I've needed to know any Latin or

German, though my vague familiarity with Latin does come in handy from time to time when I come upon unfamiliar words in something I'm reading. I occasionally tap into my memory of U.S. History, but it's not something I need on a regular basis. As for my high school Religious Studies classes,... well, let's just say that in the chaos and confusion of those post-Vatican II years, we spent a lot of time making collages, listening to John Lennon, and singing "Kumbaya." Effective post-Vatican II catechetical models had not yet been implemented to replace the <u>Baltimore Catechism</u>.

My high school English classes were certainly valuable, especially those which helped to develop my writing ability, but I think credit for my writing skills really goes to the Sisters of Mercy at Saint Gabriel School. If I remember correctly, writing was one of my strengths even before I started high school. The Sisters drilled us on correct spelling, punctuation, and grammar.

The two high school courses which stand out as the most useful for me, the two which most directly impacted my life on a daily basis, were Public Speaking and Typing. In my Public Speaking class, I was challenged to overcome my fear of speaking in front of groups. I remember how, during my elementary school years, I dreaded speaking, or even reading, in front of people. After a one-semester Public Speaking course in my freshman year, I gained both confidence and competence with speaking in front of groups.

Typing, however, stands out as the #1 course I took in high school. As an English major at Santa Clara University, my typing ability allowed me to focus on my writing skills and not worry about the mechanics of getting my words onto paper. For many of my classmates, the challenge of typing their papers was greater than that of actually writing them. I remember helping a classmate by typing several of her papers for her. Her writing skills were excellent, but she had virtually no ability to type.

I'm grateful for this skill. When I sit down to write an e-mail to a friend, I can type what I'm thinking with ease. When I was creating a worksheet, study guide, or test for my students, I was able to do so quickly and without much difficulty. And when I'm updating my blog, I can write from my heart and not struggle with the mechanics of typing. It's a simple thing, I know, yet it is a skill for which I am grateful.

Reflection Questions:

1. When you think back to your high school years, what were some of the most valuable courses you took? What made them valuable for you?

2. What skills do you utilize regularly at this point in your life which you learned in your high school years?

26

Making Wishes

> *"Once you choose hope, anything's possible."*
> ~ Christopher Reeve

*H*ave you ever picked a dandelion, made a wish, then blown all the particles away? I think most people have probably done so a time or two. I know I have. This practice leaves me with two questions: Do you really expect your wish to come true? Do dandelions actually possess some magical power?

I don't have much faith in dandelions. Personally, I don't expect wishes to come true just because I've successfully blown all the fuzz off a green stem. In fact, I don't wish for much at all. I don't spend time wishing for more money. I don't toss coins into fountains and make wishes. I don't even make a wish before blowing out birthday candles.

I do, however, have hope. I have hope for a better tomorrow. I have hope for good health for myself and my loved ones. I have hope for world peace. I hope to get along well with my family, friends, and neighbors. I hope my boys and my grandchildren find happiness and success in their lives. I hope for many things, but these are somehow different from wishes.

Wishes seem to be based on luck, whereas hope is based on faith. Hope is an unexplainable confidence that God will take care of me and those

I love. Hope is accepting whatever happens and trying to find God in both the joyful and painful experiences of life.

Devoting time, energy, and attention to prayer seems far more productive than blowing on dandelions. It may not be as cute, or as entertaining, but it certainly seems more worthwhile.

I pray every day without fail. My prayers tend to be extemporaneous, as opposed to the formal, more traditional prayers of Christianity. When I pray, I can be anywhere, doing just about anything. I don't feel the need to be on my knees or in a church building to communicate with my God. Instead, I have an ongoing conversation with God throughout each and every day.

I'm grateful for my faith, for the ability to pray, and for the sense of hope I experience each and every day. It makes my life worth living.

Reflection Questions:

1. Do you "wish" for things in your life? Do you make wishes when you toss a coin in a fountain, blow out birthday candles, or blow the fuzz off a dandelion? Do you have any expectation that these wishes will come true?

2. Do you pray? If so, when, where, why, and how do you pray? Do you have any expectations that your prayers will be answered?

3. Do you make a conscious effort to recognize God's presence in both the joyful and painful experiences in your life?

4. How does "hope" manifest itself in your life?

27

The Gift of Brokenness

"Blessings sometimes come through brokenness
that could never come in any other way."
~ Gerald May

$\mathcal{A}$t some point in time, we've all been hurt. We've all experienced the inevitable disappointments and failures of being human. We've all made mistakes we regret. We've all been victimized by betrayal, misfortune, or injustice of some kind. We've all experienced the loss of loved ones. In other words, we are all a little broken, and that's okay.

A few years ago, one of my former high school teachers recommended that I read the book *Bounce: Living the Resilient Life*, by Robert J. Wicks. When someone I respect recommends a book, I most often pick up a copy and read it. I wasn't overly impressed by this writer's style, but the book reinforced the idea that when life knocks us down, we most always have the opportunity to bounce back and turn our misfortune into something positive. This is a challenge for us all.

Life is an ongoing process of recovery. Whether the cause of our distress is self-inflicted, the result of another person's lack of sensitivity, the consequence of a random life experience, or genetics, we are challenged to find a way to acknowledge what has happened to us, to pick ourselves up, and to begin the process of healing. To sit back and feel sorry for ourselves, bitterly resenting what has happened to us, is counter-productive. To cry out that life isn't fair, while certainly a valid observation, is futile. We need to summon the strength from within to bounce back.

I've learned so many things from my friends in Japan and from Japanese culture. One lesson I learned has to do with repairing broken pottery. *Kintsukuroi* is the art of repairing pottery with gold, with the understanding that a piece of pottery is more beautiful for having been broken. The Japanese believe that when something has suffered damage and has a history, it becomes more beautiful. What a valuable lesson for all of us — that, in our brokenness, we too have the potential to become even better than we were previously.

We might, from time to time, be tempted to get down on ourselves for mistakes we've made, for failures, misfortunes, betrayals, or injustices we may have experienced. Or we might find ourselves in the thick fog of grief due to the loss of a loved one. We are challenged to find ways to heal ourselves. Just as the art of *Kintsukuroi* is practiced with the belief that a piece of pottery, in its brokenness, can become more beautiful, we must believe that we, in our brokenness, have the potential to emerge stronger and more beautiful than ever.

Reflection Questions:

1. Do you agree that, difficult as it may be, our "brokenness" can be understood as a gift?

2. Have you had a personal experience of being "broken," only to realize that, in time, you emerged stronger and better than before?

28

Recapturing Childhood Innocence

"A child can teach an adult three things:
to be happy for no reason,
to always be busy with something,
and to know how to demand with all his might
that which he desires."
~ Paulo Coelho

Recently, on her lunch break, a good friend sat outside her workplace observing children playing on the playground at the school across the street. The experience reminded her of her own younger days, when life was less complicated. She marveled at the simplicity of the children and envied the life and energy they exhibited in their play time. She then began to consider a few challenging questions:

- *Why is life so complicated for adults?*
- *Is it possible to get back to that carefree mindedness?*
- *Why do we care so much about what others think of us?*

These observations and thoughts prompted her to set a new goal for herself — to get back to that carefree state she once knew so well. She acknowledged that it's important to be responsible as an adult, but she lamented the loss of fun, running around, playing, and enjoying life. Her musings got me thinking.

There's no question that, for most people, adult life is significantly more complicated than early childhood. As we begin to take responsibility for our own lives — finding good work, being financially self-supporting, managing our time appropriately, accepting the consequences of our decisions, and handling the sometimes complicated relationships in our lives — our stress level increases proportionally. For some, the stress can be overwhelming. That's just how life works.

Is there a way we can make life a bit less stressful for ourselves? I believe there is — and it involves three components: detachment, simplicity, and gratitude. Detachment involves letting go. So many of us have such an insatiable desire to control every aspect of our lives. Sometimes it's better just to go with the flow and allow life to play out in its own way. This can certainly reduce stress. Simplicity, too, can ease the burden of day-to-day living. When we live within our means, when we refuse to buy-in to the materialistic culture in which we live, our level of stress can be reduced significantly. And, in my humble opinion, gratitude is the key to contentedness and carefree living. When we are grateful for all we have, rather than feeling deprived due to what we don't have, life improves considerably.

Finally, do others really think of us all that often? And, if so, should we care? There are times in our lives when it certainly seems that they do, but, perhaps, that's just our perception. Winston Churchill once said, *"When you're twenty, you care about what everyone thinks. When you're forty, you stop caring about what everyone thinks. When you're sixty, you realize no one was ever thinking about you in the first place."* I've certainly found this to be true. As I've gotten older, I care less about what others think of me. As a result of this simple change, I enjoy life now more than ever before. When it comes right down to it, only a handful of people truly care about us. Others are simply curious. There will, for most of us, always be some few individuals who go out of their way to bring us down. The less we respond to their negativity, the more peaceful our lives will be.

As adults, it is important for us to recognize the distinction between being childish and being childlike. There IS a difference.

Reflection Questions:

1. What life questions challenge you? Can you relate to the questions this young woman was pondering during her lunch break?

2. How would you explain the difference between "childlike" and "childish"? In what ways are you *childlike*? In what ways are you *childish*?

29

It's All About Attitude

> *"...the last of the human freedoms —*
> *to choose one's attitude*
> *in any given set of circumstances..."*
> ~ Viktor Frankl

*V*ictor Frankl was an Austrian neurologist and psychologist who managed to survive the Holocaust. Following his incarceration, he wrote of his experience in the concentration camp. His book, Man's Search for Meaning, was first published in 1946. To this day, it provides wisdom and insights to readers of all ages. I remember highlighting the quote above in my copy of Frankl's book when I was a student at Santa Clara University in 1977. Man's Search for Meaning was required reading in a Spiritual Autobiographies class. It was an excellent course in which I read an assortment of inspiring books. Frankl's book, perhaps more than any other, stands out in my memory, and this particular quote has helped me to cope with more than one challenging situation in my life.

Life doesn't always turn out the way we would hope. We often find ourselves in situations that are not to our liking. When this happens, we have choices. We can be miserable and feel sorry for ourselves. We can be unhappy and make those around us unhappy. We can pull back into our own little world and hide there until the situation is more to our liking. Or we can make a commitment to make the most of the difficult situation. The choice we make will greatly impact our attitude, and our attitude will greatly impact the choice we make. Whichever option we select, the attitude we choose is freely chosen — by us.

I know that, in my lifetime, I've made the wrong choice of attitude on multiple occasions. It's so easy to decide to be miserable and feel sorry for myself or to pull back into my own world and wait for things to get better. I've found such choices, however, to be counter-productive. While I'm waiting for the situation to improve, life is happening, and I'm missing out on it! It's so much more effective to confront a difficult situation head-on and to make it a valuable learning experience.

Over the past few years, I've made countless choices, both good and bad, pertaining to my attitude. I'm grateful for the times I've had the courage to make the better choice. And I'm hopeful that, in the future, I make the right choice more consistently.

Reflection Questions:

1. Do you agree with Frankl's quote from <u>Man's Search for Meaning</u>? In what ways might Frankl's words guide you as you live your life?

2. How do you cope with situations which are not to your liking? Do you find these coping strategies to be effective for you?

3. In your own experience, can you recall a time when your attitude affected your choice in a positive way? In a negative way?

30

Santa Cruz Lighthouse

"In order for the light to shine so brightly,
the darkness must also be present."
~ Francis Bacon

I've driven past it many times. I had the opportunity to pass it again on a sunny Labor Day weekend about ten years ago. The charming Santa Cruz lighthouse overlooks the Santa Cruz Wharf and Monterey Bay. It is, without a doubt, one of the smallest lighthouses in California, and it's definitely one of the most enchanting. On that particular weekend, I was visiting Santa Cruz with two graduates of Junshin High School in Nagasaki, Japan. We had driven down Highway 1 from Pacifica and we passed the lighthouse as we drove along West Cliff Drive on our way to the Santa Cruz Beach & Boardwalk. I explained to my guests why that particular lighthouse has such special meaning to me.

In March 2006, Yuichiro Wakiyama, a teacher of English at Junshin High School in Nagasaki, stayed at our home during his homestay visit to California. He and I had become good friends a year or two before when, on his first homestay visit to America, he stayed at the home of one of my students. At one point during that visit, the parents of his host family had a previous commitment to attend an out-of-town weekend

101

event. Because of that commitment, I had offered to spend the weekend with Yuichiro, showing him around the San Francisco Bay Area.

One of our weekend outings took us over the hill to Santa Cruz, on the coast of Monterey Bay. We enjoyed a relaxing lunch at Gilda's Restaurant on the wharf. From our seats in the restaurant, we could clearly see the Santa Cruz lighthouse perched on the cliff above the surf. After lunch, we visited some of the shops along the wharf. In one of the shops, I found miniature replicas of the Santa Cruz lighthouse. Most people who know me well are aware that I like lighthouses, so I wanted to add the Santa Cruz lighthouse to my collection. Instead of purchasing only one, however, I bought two — one for myself and one for Yuichiro.

When I presented the lighthouse to him as a gift, I told Yuichiro that I would keep mine on my desk in my classroom as a remembrance of our friendship and the good times we had spent together. He assured me that he would keep his lighthouse on his desk at Junshin in Nagasaki. Now that I am retired, my Santa Cruz lighthouse sits on my desk in my home office.

I treasure the memory, the lighthouse, and my friendship with Yuichiro. We've shared many good times together in California and Nagasaki. When Kathy and I visited Japan over spring break in April 2007, and again when we brought a group of fourteen students to Nagasaki in October 2013, we enjoyed delightful dinners with Yuichiro and his wife, Kuniko.

In my retirement, I doubt that I will be visiting Nagasaki again soon. In spite of this, I am confident that my friendship with Yuichiro will continue to flourish. He's my Japanese brother and I cherish our friendship.

Reflection Questions:

1. Do you have a memento which reminds you of a specific person? What is it about this item, or this person, that makes the memento so special to you?

2. Do you happen to have a favorite lighthouse somewhere in the United States or elsewhere in the world? What is it about this structure which makes it special for you?

31

Carpe Diem

*"One day you will wake up
and there won't be any more time
to do the things you've always wanted to do."*
~ Paulo Coelho

$\mathcal{W}$hat makes a day extraordinary? What makes a life extraordinary? I'm confident that the varied responses to these questions could fill more than a few pages. Most of us, I would guess, would not describe our life as extraordinary. It seems that most of us consider ourselves to be normal folks doing normal things. We get up in the morning, eat breakfast, go to work, eat lunch, work a bit more, return home, eat dinner, spend some time with family, perhaps watch a little television or do some reading, then go to bed. If we're conscientious, we set aside a little time each day for exercise and prayer. Hardly extraordinary, right?

I think most of us would prefer to live a life which is, at least, somewhat extraordinary. We'd like to be happy. We'd like to savor each day of our existence and make the most of our time on this earth. Unfortunately, for many of us, complacency sets in, depriving us of the opportunity to live life to the fullest. We take each day for granted, falsely believing that we are guaranteed another day tomorrow.

Much has been written about the secret of living a happy life. One recipe for doing so is to accept where we are in life and to make the most out of every day with which we are blessed. Sometimes, as we anticipate events in our future, it's easy for us to count the days, while failing to make those days count. The Buddha warned us about this when he said, *"The trouble is, you think you have time."*

Complacency is like a disease. We often take our days for granted. We wait, hoping for the perfect day, the perfect job opportunity, or the perfect relationship to suddenly become a reality in our life. Perhaps, rather than waiting and hoping, we should take the initiative to do everything within our power to make each day as perfect as possible, and to make our job or our current relationship as perfect as we possibly can. Like the Buddha, Mother Teresa also urged us to *seize the day*. She reminded us, *"Yesterday is gone. Tomorrow has not yet come. We have only today."*

Seize the day — *carpe diem*. I recall hearing this term mentioned at the funeral service for Richard Jatta, the father of one of my former students. He had lost his battle with cancer at a very young age, leaving his wife and two children behind. He knew, all too well, the meaning of *carpe diem*. It's unfortunate that we often recognize and appreciate the value of each day only when we learn that our days are numbered. In his final days on earth, Rich learned to love each day, a practice we should all embrace.

Carpe diem is an opportunity which presents itself to us each and every day. The challenge is to recognize this opportunity and to make the most of it.

Like Richard, it is quite possible that many of our loved ones came to a greater understanding of, and appreciation for, the concept of *carpe diem* at the end of their lives. Robin Williams, in the movie *Dead Poets Society*, urged us to listen to their voices: *"If you listen real close, you can *hear them whisper their legacy to you. Go on, lean in. Listen, you hear it? Carpe diem, seize the day, boys. Make your lives extraordinary."*

Reflection Questions:

1. In what way(s) do you see your own life as extraordinary?

2. How might recognizing the extraordinary nature of your life change the way you live your life?

3. What do you think of the Paulo Coelho quote at the beginning of this entry? What is it that you've always wanted to do?

32

An Embarrassing Moment

"It's okay to not be perfect.
It's okay to make mistakes."
~ Dawn Stanyon

*T*hanks to the wonders of Facebook, my recent reacquaintance with several elementary school classmates has brought back a flood of memories of people and experiences, both good and bad, from my days at Saint Gabriel School in San Francisco. As my wife, Kathy, and I discussed some of the online conversations I've been having with these friends from my past, Kathy took the opportunity to remind me of one of her favorite stories from my days at Saint Gabriel, a memory I shared with her many years ago.

Her name was Eileen. She was one of my seventh-grade classmates and, for reasons I never understood since I was such a likable kid, she despised me. She was consistently antagonistic towards me, so, not surprisingly, I wasn't overly fond of her either. I was less than excited when Sister Marian Corita, our seventh-grade teacher, introduced a Secret Santa gift exchange among the students and I drew Eileen's name.

Despite the fact that I was a mere twelve years old, I looked upon this situation as an opportunity to turn an enemy into a friend. So I

109

headed out to GETs (the acronym for *Government Employees Together*, a discount membership shopping center located just a few blocks from my home) to select a Christmas gift that I would be proud to present to her.

I knew that girls like jewelry, so I headed over to that section of the store to check out necklaces. I don't recall how long it took, but after wandering around for awhile, I eventually found what I thought might be a pleasing, peace-making gift. It was a string of pearls, or perhaps something that looked like pearls, since I had a limited budget. Little did I know, at the time, that I had strayed just a little outside the Jewelry Department and into the Optometry Department. It was there that I found what I thought would be the perfect gift.

The day of the Secret Santa gift exchange arrived. I was excited, and confident that I'd selected a gift which would impress Eileen and change her opinion of me forever. I watched with great anticipation as she unwrapped the gift and opened the box. Her reaction was not what I had expected.

"This is SO stupid!" she announced with hostility to our classmates sitting around her. "I don't even wear glasses!"

I guess I hadn't noticed that, rather than a clasp to hold the ends of the necklace together, the string of pearls I purchased had two loops, one at each end, through which the user could thread the frame of a pair of reading glasses. It wasn't a necklace at all!

Needless to say, this incident didn't do much to repair my relationship with Eileen, nor did it improve my status among my classmates. I was absolutely humiliated, and Eileen made no effort to ease the discomfort of this embarrassing moment.

It may seem strange to say that I'm grateful for this experience, but I really am. First of all, it taught me a lesson about humility. Secondly, it helped me learn to be a bit more careful when shopping for a gift. And finally, it has provided a humorous, entertaining, true story to share with others for the past fifty years. Two life lessons and five decades of entertainment — all for only about $2.49. Such a deal!

Reflection Questions:

1. What was the most embarrassing experience of your childhood? How did you cope with the situation?

2. Are you able to look back on embarrassing or difficult moments in your lifetime with a sense of genuine gratitude for lessons learned?

33

Coping with Change

"It is not the strongest of the species that survives,
nor the most intelligent,
but the one most responsive to change."
~ Charles Darwin

It is often said that the only two certainties in life are death and taxes. I disagree. Another reality we can always count on is change.

Life is full of transitions — childhood to adolescence, adolescence to young adulthood, ignorant to educated, young to old, day to night,... The list could go on and on. Some of the changes which take place in our lives are fairly easy to accept. Others, however, can turn our lives upside down. Coping with change can be quite a challenge.

One of the changes I've been dealing with for several years now has to do with my relationships with my three sons. I certainly wasn't the perfect parent in their formative years. I made my fair share of parenting mistakes, though I'm confident that I was a good Dad and that I did the best job I possibly could have done. In recent years, however, our relationships have changed. No longer do they need the type of father I was for them when they were younger. No longer do they need me to manage their lives. All three of my sons have become increasingly competent young adults and, for the most part, are able to manage just about every aspect of their own lives. As this growth in maturity took place, I had a choice. I could have attempted to continue to parent them as I did when they were younger, and, in doing so, become parentally obsolete. I also had the option to adapt to the changes in their lives — clearly the better choice.

As adolescents become young adults, it's essential that parents acknowledge what's happening in their lives, and to make a significant adjustment. Over the years, my role with all three of my sons changed from being their manager to being their mentor. Most of the important decisions in their lives are now theirs to make, not mine. My role is to simply be there for them, support them, listen to them, and serve as a sounding board when they ask for feedback on a particular issue. It's a role to which I am still adapting.

I'm sure situations might still arise from time to time which cause me to temporarily revert back to my manager role, but it's been quite awhile since I've had to do that. The guys are doing well. They're all gainfully employed. All three seem happy, focused, and generally content with their lives. I want them to know that I will always be here for them. At the same time, however, I need them to realize that I trust them implicitly and that I'm confident in their ability to take care of themselves.

Life is full of transitions. It is essential, therefore, that we learn to cope effectively with the changes which confront us.

Reflection Questions:

1. What transition in your life presented you with the greatest challenge? How did you deal with this challenge?

2. Generally speaking, do you deal effectively with changes in your life? What strategies might you employ to improve your coping skills?

34

A Matter of Perspective

*"Inside yourself or outside,
you never have to change what you see,
only the way you see it."*
~ Thaddeus Golas

*F*rom time to time, we encounter a situation and immediately jump to a conclusion about it. Maybe it's a problem at work. Perhaps, it has to do with a family member, friend, or coworker. I'm guessing that most people, at one time or another, have formulated an opinion about a situation or a person only to learn at a later date that their perception was inaccurate or somehow flawed. It's a common experience.

The quote above, by the Polish-American writer, Thaddeus Golas, provides some food for thought, especially if you apply it to the concept of gratitude. Imagine this: If a person walks into a dark room and does not know where to turn on the light, the person may leave the room believing that the room is empty, for he did not see anything inside the room. If, on the other hand, that same person were to re-enter the room and turn on the light, his perception would be quite different. Nothing inside the room changed, other than the person's ability to see what he could not see before.

Sometimes we go through life without turning on the lights. Therefore, we fail to recognize all the things for which we could be grateful. Nothing is really different, it's just that when we turn on the lights, we become aware of what is already there.

Maybe that's why some people can live a life of contentment, while others feel constantly deprived. Their situations may be quite similar, but one sees with the light of gratitude while the other is blinded by the darkness of their own expectations or, perhaps, the expectations of society.

Staying focused on the many ways we have been blessed allows us to see clearly. It's true, life is not perfect. Living a life of gratitude, however, empowers us to experience each new day with a refreshing perspective.

Reflection Questions:

1. Can you recall a time when you formulated an opinion about a situation or a person only to learn at a later date that your perception was inaccurate or somehow flawed?

2. How might you change your outlook on life simply by changing your perspective to a focus on gratitude?

3. Can you recall a situation when, even though nothing had changed, your perception of the situation improved considerably simply due to a shift in the way you chose to look at it?

35

Experiencing God in the Ordinary

*"The gift of darkness draws you
to know God's presence beyond what
thought, imagination, or sensory feeling
can comprehend."*
- Richard Rohr

During the 1974-75 academic year, when I was teaching at a catholic high school in the Bahamas, I got to know a young man who was considering a vocation to the Benedictine Order. He was a native Bahamian, living as a novice in the monastery and working with the maintenance crew at Saint Augustine's College. He spent many hours each day on the campus of the seventh through twelfth grade school. Due to the fact that he was discerning a religious vocation, he wore the traditional white robe worn by the other Benedictine monks.

One Friday after school, one of my ninth-grade students came to visit me in my classroom. She was visibly shaken and said she needed to talk to me about something important. When I inquired what that might be, she removed three white envelopes from her purse and placed them on my desk. The envelopes contained three letters — torrid love letters — written to her by this member of the Benedictine community. He had given the letters to her over a period of days in the previous weeks.

She asked me what she should do. With her permission, I took the letters and assure her that I would deal with the situation over the weekend.

The next day, in the early afternoon, I put the letters in my back pocket and exited my room, which was located in a building adjacent to the monastery. I was planning to give them to my immediate supervisor, who also happened to be the Prior of the Benedictine community. I believed that it was his responsibility to handle the situation. As I approached the side door of the monastery, the door opened and the young brother-in-training emerged. I stopped, looked directly into his eyes, and, without hesitation, said to him, "We need to talk." He asked me what we needed to talk about. I pulled the letters from my back pocket and said, "These." He was stunned.

I honestly had not expected to confront him. I had no desire whatsoever to address this situation on my own. I thought it would be best if my supervisor handled it, but in the moment, confronting him with the evidence seemed like the right thing to do. I honestly don't remember exactly what I said to the man, but I vividly recall walking away at the conclusion of our brief conversation and being absolutely overwhelmed with the feeling that I'd just been used by God to convey a critical message to this obviously confused young man. I remember thinking that what I had said was exactly what needed to be said, even though I had not prepared to say anything to him. For some unexplained reason, the words just came out perfectly. To this day, I am convinced that those were not my words.

One of the greatest challenges in life is to recognize God in the ordinary — to experience God's presence in the day-to-day happenings of our life. The ability to do so begins with an openness to the possibility that God actually can and does become present to us at critical times. I'm especially grateful for the experiences when this has happened in my life.

Reflection Questions:

1. Have you ever had an overwhelming sense of God's presence at a particular moment in your life?

2. Have you ever had the feeling that God "used" you to accomplish a specific task?

3. Can you recall a time when you unexpectedly, yet effectively, dealt with a complicated situation? Did you have a sense of the presence of God at that time?

36

The Gift of Visualization

*"See things as you would have them be
instead of as they are."*
~ Robert Collier

I first learned about visualization in January 1980 when I attended a workshop on junior high counseling at Santa Clara University. While the emphasis of the workshop focused on ways to use visualization to enhance a student's academic achievement, I explored another use for it.

The day following the workshop, my eighth grade girls' basketball team from Saint Christopher School would play their first game of the season. These girls had lost every game they'd ever played in fifth through seventh grades. As I listened to how visualization could be used to increase a student's success in the classroom, I was considering how I could apply the concept to the basketball court.

The next day, the girls arrived at Piedmont Hills High School for their game with Saint Victor School, the team which had won the league championship in fifth through seventh grades. Fortunately, I didn't know anything about the Saint Victor team prior to the game. About fifteen minutes before tip-off, I gathered my team together to lead them through a process of relaxation and visualization. The girls thought it was sort of strange, at first, but they participated actively. Then they took the court for their game. Much to everyone's surprise, they defeated the team from Saint Victor 38-16 — the first of eight consecutive league victories and a league championship. Relaxation and visualization became our pre-game ritual throughout the season.

The quote above by Robert Collier, one of America's original authors on the topic of success, encapsulates what visualization is all about: creating a vision of a preferred outcome — and then achieving it.

When my oldest son, Tom, was playing his first season of Little League baseball in 1994, he was hit in the back by a pitch during his first at-bat of the season. Understandably, he was reluctant to stay in the batter's box for the next eight or nine games. My wife, Kathy, suggested that I use visualization with him prior to his next game. I did. In that game, Tom got his first base hit of the season in his first at-bat, and two more hits in subsequent plate appearances. Then, with two outs in the bottom of the last inning, the bases loaded, and his team down by two runs, Tom came to the plate. He hit a solid line drive which landed perfectly between the left- and center-fielders and rolled to the fence. All three baserunners scored. The Yankees had won their first game. Tom stood on second base wondering why everyone was walking off the field!

Yes, visualization is powerful. It is a tool which has the potential to help us in many aspects of our lives. I will always be grateful to have this tool at my disposal.

Reflection Questions:

1. Do you believe that you increase your chances of achieving an outcome by visualizing such an outcome?

2. Have you ever had an experience of visualization which contributed to achieving a preferred outcome for yourself or others?

37

A Commitment to Excellence

"Excellence is doing ordinary things
extraordinarily well."
~ John W. Gardner

When it comes to professional football, I've always been more of a San Francisco 49ers fan than an Oakland Raiders fan. Both are San Francisco Bay Area teams. In baseball, I feel comfortable rooting for both the local National League team, the Giants, and the local American League team, the A's. When it comes to football, however, while I support the 49ers, I just don't have any connection whatsoever with the Raiders. Despite this, I have always been impressed with the Raiders motto: *"A Commitment to Excellence."*

I guess I'd be deceiving myself if I didn't admit that I'm a bit of a perfectionist. I'm well-aware that this is not necessarily a good thing. I know I drive some people crazy. I also know it is problematic when I project my need for perfection onto others. I've done this. Not surprisingly, it makes for difficult relationships with the people around me. I'm not sure where such feelings originate. I certainly wasn't a perfectionist when I was in elementary school or high school. It wasn't until I started Santa Clara University that I began to exhibit symptoms of this disability.

I'm not perfect. Not only is this clearly evident to others, it's clear to me, too. I do, however, possess a commitment to excellence. I wanted to be an excellent teacher during my years in the classroom. I strive to be an excellent husband, father, and grandfather. I work hard to be an excellent writer. It's important for me to manage our family finances with a degree of excellence. During the years when I coordinated a Japan Exchange Program at the high school where I was teaching, I wanted to do that with excellence, too. I have very high expectations of myself and others. But there is a significant difference between excellence and perfection.

Excellence is putting forth 100% effort, regardless of the outcome. Excellence is doing the best one can possibly do in any given situation. Even when things don't turn out the way one might like, it is possible to experience a sense of personal satisfaction if we know we've put forth our very best effort.

I sleep well at night. One reason for this is that I am reasonably confident that I'm doing the best possible job I can in my life. I make mistakes. I occasionally disappoint people. Some people don't like me. I can't let these things get in the way. All I can do is consistently put forth my best effort, constantly strive for excellence, and hope that what I've done is enough. I'm grateful for this drive in my life. Even though it might be bothersome to some people around me, I'm comfortable with the way I am. I can only hope that all my relationships are characterized by mutual respect and understanding.

Reflection Questions:

1. Do you have experience coping with perfectionism in yourself or in those around you? What strategies do you employ for dealing with this challenge?

2. Are you comfortable falling short of expectations when you know in your heart that you have put forth your absolute best effort in the endeavor?

3. Is a "commitment to excellence" evident in your life?

38

Sprezzatura

*"Be like a duck. Calm on the surface,
but always paddling like the dickens underneath."*
~ Michael Caine

*T*iger Woods made it look so simple in the early years of his professional golf career. He was cool under pressure. He was incredibly confident in his ability to play the game. He performed at a level which far surpassed the average golfer. Anyone who has ever attempted to hit a golf ball knows how challenging it can be, yet Woods made hitting a 400-yard drive down the center of the fairway look second-natured. He had sprezzatura!

Sprezzatura is an Italian word which refers to the art of making a difficult task look easy. The term means to work at performing an action with the outward appearance of effortless grace. Ted Williams had it in baseball. Joe Montana and Jerry Rice displayed it in football. Michael Jordan, and now Steph Curry, played with it, too. It's an enviable quality.

I was introduced to the concept of sprezzatura in a Renaissance Literature class at Santa Clara University in 1978. It was a characteristic of the ideal Renaissance Man, one who displayed above-average competence as a scholar, athlete, or warrior, yet made it all look effortless.

The word does not imply that any of the athletes mentioned above put forth less than 100% effort in their respective sport. In fact, it's probably safe to say that all of them worked harder than the average athlete to develop the skills they displayed on the field of competition. Because of their impressive work ethic, and the gift of sprezzatura, they were able to perform challenging tasks with incredible grace and ease.

During my years in the classroom, I attempted to teach with sprezzatura. I tried to present information to my students in such a way that it appeared natural, even effortless. In reality, however, I devoted countless hours of preparation in order to do that. I organized myself in such a way that I was always well-prepared, if not over-prepared. When showing a video clip, I would always take the time to cue the tape to the exact starting point before class began, so as not to waste class time doing so. I stayed up late at night grading tests and papers so that I could return them to my students the next day. I kept the classroom environment neat, clean, and orderly. Class presentations were always well-organized. To my students and colleagues, it may have appeared that it all happened so easily for me. They just never saw the behind-the-scenes effort I invested to make it happen.

Sprezzatura does not come easy. Certainly, a person must be blessed with a certain ability level, but that, in itself, does not suffice. The amount of effort one combines with that level of ability is what enables a person to perform a task in such a way that it appears to be effortless to others.

I am grateful for the comfort level I experienced in the classroom throughout my teaching career. I'm equally grateful for the motivation I had to put forth the effort to teach well, and, yes, to make it look effortless.

Reflection Questions:

1. Who have you observed that performs their job in such a way that they make a difficult task look effortless? Is the task truly easier for this person, or would you acknowledge that, to accomplish the task, s/he clearly put forth a high level of effort, even if behind the scenes?

2. Do you have sprezzatura? Is there any particular task or activity in which you engage which appears to others to be effortless for you, even though you work very hard to accomplish the task?

39

Friendships

*"Sometimes you put walls up
not to keep people out,
but to see who cares enough
to break them down."*
~ Socrates

Friendship is something most people don't spend a lot of time thinking about. I know I don't. I've gone through most of my life taking my friendships for granted. I remember when I met my wife, Kathy, her sister, Clare, and a number of other young adults from my parish church back in 1984. It seemed that wherever we went — the Santa Cruz Beach & Boardwalk, the local mall, Candlestick Park in San Francisco, etc. — I'd run into people I knew. I remember someone mentioning that they were amazed at how many friends I had. Yes, I knew a lot of people, but were they really my friends?

One of the chapters in the text book I used with my senior high school students focused on the topic of friendship. The book made several thought-provoking points on the subject, but none more challenging than the distinction for many men between friends and acquaintances. It seems so easy for some men to be friends with women, yet I'm left to wonder if men can really be friends with other men — or if, perhaps, we are limited to the status of acquaintances.

Acquaintances fall into a variety of categories: buddies, collaborators, relatives, and neighbors, to name a few. I have no shortage of guys I know who fall into these categories. I have buddies who I talk with occasionally, and every now and then, we'll get together for a meal or to watch a baseball game. Throughout my life, I've also had many collaborators. These were colleagues in the workplace or, perhaps, neighbors with whom I worked on a neighborhood project. In so many cases, we worked together, but that was the extent of our relationship. We didn't really know each other well, and we didn't see each other outside of a particular collaborative environment. And, of course, I have relatives. But the reality of the situation is that I see them only at family gatherings such as weddings and funerals, or occasional family dinners. Rarely do we just get together to be together.

Finally, I have neighbors. Having lived in the same home for more than thirty years, I've had the opportunity to get to know several other men who live in our condominium complex. Unfortunately, I know little about them other than their names and what type of work they do. Our contact is often limited to those times when we happen to bump into each other at the pool, mailbox, or trash bins.

So yes, I know many guys, but they are mostly acquaintances. It took me awhile, but I finally acknowledged this to myself. When I think of what a true friend is, I'm confronted with the reality that, while I do have many acquaintances, I have very few true friends. It is a humbling realization. True friendships need to be nurtured, and, through the years, I have done little to allow many potential true friendships to thrive. For some reason, I decided a long time ago that it was easier, or safer, perhaps, to just keep my relationships with other guys at the acquaintance level. In some ways, this is unfortunate. I do believe, however, that such is the case with many men.

I am grateful for those few men in my life I can call true friends. They know who they are. They know that I make an effort to sustain my relationships with them. And I know I have work to do in this area of my life.

Reflection Questions:

1. Do you agree that friendships between men are significantly different than most friendships between women? Why do you think this is the case?

2. If you are male, what can you do to better nurture your relationships with other men? If you are female, what might you do to help a significant man in your life to nurture his relationships with other guys?

3. Is there someone in your life who, in the past, you considered to be a very close friend, but with whom you've allowed the relationship to fade away? Have you considered attempting to reconnect with this person?

40

A Lifetime of Writing

*"Writing means sharing.
It's part of the human condition to want to share things —
thoughts, ideas, opinions."*
- Paulo Coelho

$\mathcal{I}$ am well-aware that, for many people, writing does not come easy. Composing a simple letter can be a burdensome, time-consuming, and often overwhelming task. I have not engaged in, nor have I read, any research on why this is such a common experience, but I'm sure such research must exist. From time to time, I think about why writing has been, and continues to be, such an enjoyable undertaking for me. A few possibilities come to mind.

First of all, I attended Saint Gabriel Elementary School in San Francisco, where the Sisters of Mercy set a high bar for the quality of student writing. Spelling, grammar, punctuation, and neatness were priorities for all written assignments. I graduated from eighth grade with a solid foundation in the art of writing.

In those same years, my mother stressed the importance of writing thank you notes for all occasions — birthdays, Christmas, First Communion, Confirmation, and graduation. I quickly learned that it was best to write a high-quality note the first time, since failure to do so would mean doing it over again. As in school, correct grammar, spelling, and punctuation were expected. So, too, was good penmanship.

My eighth grade teacher, Sister Mary Brigid, had taught in a catholic elementary school in Imperial Beach, California before coming to Saint Gabriel for our final year. She thought it would be a good idea to initiate a pen pal program between her current eighth grade students and the students she had taught as seventh graders at Saint Charles School the previous year. My pen pal, Sue Groff, and I exchanged letters for at least five or six years. While these letters were not checked for quality by an adult, we knew by then what was expected of us in all our writing.

During my four years at Saint Ignatius College Prep, my classmates and I did a considerable amount of writing in all subject areas. Teachers in history, science, and religious studies classes had the same high standards for writing as our English teachers. In all these courses, we practiced the various styles of writing we learned in our English classes: creative, persuasive, argumentative, narrative, compare/contrast, and research.

By the time I got to Santa Clara University, where I majored in English with an emphasis in writing, I was a confident writer. As I had experienced in my high school years, a significant amount of writing was required across the curriculum, and the same high quality of written work was expected regardless of the subject matter.

Since December 2006, I've devoted a fair amount of time to writing on my *Attitude of Gratitude* blog. Doing so has been therapeutic. There is absolutely no stress involved in my writing projects. If I feel like writing on a particular day, I write. If not, I don't. But when I write, I try to do so with the same level of conscientiousness with which I wrote academic papers throughout my formal education. To me, there's only one way to write, and that's to write well.

I will always be grateful to my mother, and to the teachers I had at every level, for encouraging me to write, and for setting such high standards for my written work.

Reflection Questions:

1. Do you enjoy writing or is it a constant challenge for you to put your thoughts into words?

2. Is there anything in particular that you would like to write — a book, a memoir, a letter to a friend? What prevents you from doing so?

3. Have you ever considered keeping a journal of your thoughts, questions, and feelings? Does the thought of starting a *Gratitude Journal* appeal to you?

41

Cultural Diversity

"Multiculturalism:
the preservation of different cultures or cultural identities
within a unified society, as in a state or nation."
~ Random House Dictionary

When I first visited Nagasaki, Japan in 1998, I took four high school students, three Filipino-American students and one Caucasian, for a two-week homestay experience. A few days into our visit, two Japanese students approached me in the courtyard. One of the girls said, "Kevin sensei, we are very surprised. We thought you would bring American students to Japan."

A bit surprised by their statement, I assured them that I had most certainly done so. The student responded, "No. Only one!"

In Nagasaki, Japanese people, with few exceptions, are born in Japan. They look and sound Japanese. Their actions reflect the rich tradition of Japanese culture. So when these students told me that only one of the four students I brought to Japan was American, I couldn't help but consider the question: What does an American look like?

On subsequent visits to Nagasaki, my students directly addressed the topic of multiculturalism in presentations to Japanese students in their English classes. They explained that, in America, just about everyone is from somewhere else. The population of the United States includes Irish-Americans, Italian-Americans, Polish-, Chinese-, Filipino-, and African-Americans, just to name a few. This was a very foreign concept for the students in Nagasaki. They have virtually no experience with multiculturalism in their community.

Schools throughout the Santa Clara Valley, where I've lived for most of my adult life, have been gifted with cultural diversity for many years. We have a sizable Filipino population. There are many Latino students. We have students from Portugal, Croatia, Guatemala, India, Pakistan, Germany, England, Iran, Vietnam, and many other countries. These students have much to offer our school communities. From time to time, most Silicon Valley schools integrate traditions from various cultures into school assemblies and celebrations.

I'm grateful for the diverse gifts these young people have to share. I learned so much about other cultures from the students I taught through the years. In the school where I taught for thirty-one years, students were not identified by their race or culture. All were valued members of our diverse community, and the cultural differences were acknowledged and celebrated.

Reflection Questions:

1. What was your experience of multiculturalism in the schools you attended as a young person? Was cultural diversity a reality in those schools?

2. What is your own cultural background? Were you able to share traditions from your culture with your classmates and teachers in your formative years?

3. Do you perceive the cultural diversity which exists in the United States today to be a gift, a challenge, or both?

42

"There, but for the Grace of God..."

*"Some people are born on third base,
but they go through life thinking they've hit a triple."*
~ Barry Switzer

$\mathcal{B}$arry Switzer was a football guy. He made a name for himself as the head football coach of the Oklahoma Sooners and Dallas Cowboys. A few years ago, I came across the quote above attributed to him. Surprisingly, it refers to baseball, rather than football. Although Coach Switzer was never one of my favorite sports personalities, this quote is one of my favorites.

I shared these words of wisdom with my students on many occasions. They liked the message and they understood it. They were often exposed to evidence of the reality of which it speaks. Some students I taught were born into extreme wealth, not an unusual situation in a private high school. While most of these students realized how fortunate they were, and realized that the wealth they enjoyed was not of their making, some few displayed the attitude Coach Switzer described. They seemed to think they were better than those around them because they drove a nicer car, lived in the right neighborhood, or owned the latest must-have items from the mall. It's not uncommon to find such an attitude among some students.

I am well aware of how fortunate I was to be born into a family of relative affluence. I say "relative" affluence because our family certainly wasn't wealthy in my childhood. Compared to the wealth that exists in the United States today, I would still describe my family of origin as middle-class, at best. The financial security we enjoyed was due to the hard work of my father. Working as many as three jobs at some points in his life, he did what had to be done to provide for our family.

The financial security I've experienced throughout my lifetime is primarily due to the fact that I was born into a family in which life's essentials were provided for me. I had a comfortable childhood home. I received an excellent catholic school education. I had first-rate health care. Transportation to school or other activities was most often available, as needed. I had opportunities which enabled me to grow as a person. Was I standing on third base? Absolutely! But one thing I know for sure — I didn't hit the triple.

One of my goals in the courses I taught to high school students was to help them become aware of how blessed they were — and to help them develop a sense of genuine gratitude, as well as true compassion, for those who lack the basic necessities of life. I wanted them to understand that it is only through the grace of God that we enjoy the lifestyle we experience, and that we have a moral responsibility to care for those who are less fortunate. As my mother said so often in my youth, "There, but for the grace of God, go I."

Reflection Questions:

1. What are your thoughts about Barry Switzer's quote. Have you personally encountered people who take credit for being on third base when they were not the one who hit the triple? How do you cope with such individuals?

2. Do you agree that those of us who have been blessed with all we need have a moral obligation to actively and compassionately respond to those who are unable to provide for their own needs?

43

Losing My Dad

"By the time a man realizes that his father was right,
he has a son who thinks he's wrong."
~ Charles Wadsworth

The placement of this post as #43 in this book is not random. My Dad was a graduate of the Saint Ignatius High School (San Francisco) class of 1943. His favorite number was 43. And when he earned the rank of Battalion Chief in the San Francisco Fire Department, his badge number was 43. It's interesting to note that in today's "texting" jargon, "43" means "love you."

My Dad passed away unexpectedly on the night of Thursday, July 31, 2008. It was the Feast of Saint Ignatius of Loyola — Dad's favorite saint. His death was quite unexpected. He sustained major head trauma when he fell down the stairs of our family home in San Francisco. He was 82.

For years, I had been telling people that nothing prepares us for the death of our own parent. After my Dad's passing, I know first-hand that this is absolutely true. Despite my efforts to prepare myself for this inevitable event, when I got the call from my Mom telling me that Dad had fallen, and that "it doesn't look good," I found myself a bit disoriented. In the days and weeks after his death, I was at a loss to truly comprehend how I felt. One minute I'd be fine, acknowledging the inevitability of death. The next minute I'd be in tears, wondering how I was going to cope with such a devastating loss in my life.

The relationship between father and son is a complicated one. I've tried my best in recent years to understand it — as both a son and as a father to my three sons.

In the late 1980's, KCBS radio in San Francisco aired a short-lived Sunday night program called "Man to Man." It was a call-in talk show for men to discuss men's issues. Given that goal, I guess it's no surprise that the program was short-lived!

I recall one specific evening — it was Fathers' Day. The host pointed out that many listeners were not fathers themselves, so he did not want to talk about the experience of being a father. The one thing all listeners had in common was that we all had fathers. He acknowledged that, for some, their father might no longer be alive or a part of their life, for whatever reason, but we all have or had fathers. So the host asked listeners to call in to answer a simple two-part question: "If you could spend fifteen minutes in conversation with your father, (1) what one thing would you tell him, and (2) what one thing would you ask him?"

Throughout the two-hour program, responses to the first part of the question were split about 50/50 between "I love you" and "I hate you." There seemed to be very little middle-ground on this part of the question. The second half of the question had much more agreement in the responses. Approximately 90% of callers said they would ask their father the same question. There were several variations of the question, but basically they all wanted to know the same thing: "Are you proud of me?" or "Do you approve of what I'm doing with my life?"

Men desperately want and need the approval of their father. I know I did. When I think back to my young adult days, I know my Dad was disappointed in me on two occasions: (1) when I decided not to stay in the Jesuits after less than six months in the Novitiate, and (2) when, after passing the test and making the list for the San Francisco Fire Department, I declined the job to accept a position teaching middle school literature in San José. That one was difficult for him to understand and accept.

The day before my Dad died, I had returned from a business trip to Washington, D.C. I'd tried to call home early the next morning, but Mom and Dad had not yet returned from morning Mass. I tried again around 5:30 in the afternoon. Again no answer. An hour later, my phone rang. Mom and I talked for quite awhile, as we often did. Then I spoke with Dad. My conversation with him was much longer than usual. He wanted to know all about the meeting I attended in D.C. At the end of our conversation, he said something I will never forget. His last words to me, "I love you, and I'm very proud of you," will stay with me for as long as I live. For this, and for the gift Dad was to me for the first fifty-four years of my life, I am tremendously grateful.

Reflection Questions:

1. Can anything truly prepare us for the loss of a parent or other loved one?

2. How would you describe your relationship with your own father? Did you feel the need to know that he loved you? That he was proud of you?

3. If you could have a 15-minute conversation with your father, what one thing would you tell him? What one thing would you ask him?

44

Goin' Out to Play

"G'bye. I'm going out to play."
~ Shel Silverstein

Growing up in the 1960's was a very different experience than growing up today. Sure there are technological differences, but that's not my point. When I was a kid growing up in The City, I'd head home after school, change out of my school uniform, and "go out to play." It was quite simple.

Where did we play? Well, we had several choices. South Sunset Playground was the obvious venue, located just two blocks west of our home. I spent hours there as a child playing on the swings, slides, and monkey bars. As I got older, I'd play basketball, tennis, or strikeouts with other guys in the neighborhood. I also played on several soccer and baseball teams which claimed South Sunset as our home field.

Not all of our playtime was spent at the playground. One of my favorite play areas was the strip of trees and bushes on the west side of Sunset Boulevard between Vicente and Wawona Streets. If my memory serves me well, there were more trees back in the '60's than are there today. One of the trees, fairly close to Wawona Street, featured a tree house made of wood planks. I don't know who built it or when, but it provided an awesome fort for those of us who played there. I remember playing in the boulevard trees with Rick Blake, Dave Dixon, Mike Cilia, and many other guys from the neighborhood. We would play "army," or "police," or any number of other games. Sometimes we would just hang out and talk. Our time was unstructured, but we always enjoyed our time together.

It seems that kids today are missing out on that kind of play time. For a variety of reasons, parents today provide much more structured play time for their kids. The concept of "goin' out to play" seems to be a thing of the past. Parents now cart their kids off to karate classes, Little League baseball, "play dates" with other kids the same age, or to any number of other organized activities. To an extent these activities can be good and healthy, but many kids today are being deprived of using their imagination to create games for themselves. Make-believe games were part of the fun of growing up in my early years. Whether we were in our backyard, at the playground, in the boulevard trees, or just out in the street on 38th Avenue, neighborhood kids were quite inventive in coming up with games which kept us engaged and entertained for hours on end.

I know child safety is a major concern of parents today, which is why parents are less inclined to allow their kids to just "go out and play." Parents want to know that their kids are safe at all times. Unfortunately, that overprotection, and the resulting lack of freedom, combined with the addiction many kids today have to video and computer games, has led to a generation of young people who are dependent on their parents well beyond the early adolescent years. It has also led to a generation of kids for whom obesity is a major health crisis.

Children growing up today have so many things my generation didn't have, but I wouldn't trade growing up in the '60's for anything. Playing kick-the-can or hide-and-seek with the neighborhood kids after dinner during the summer months was a wonderful experience. So, too, was playing make-believe games throughout the neighborhood. We always had a lot of fun — and I'm grateful for that!

Reflection Questions:

1. What memories do you have of going outside to play? Did you experience the freedom to explore your neighborhood with your friends?

2. What is your favorite, or most memorable, childhood experience?

3. How might parents today provide their children with opportunities for creative, unstructured play time while still providing the safety those children need today?

45

Being There Totally

"Yesterday is history, tomorrow is a mystery,
today is a gift of God, which is why we call it the present."
~ Bil Keane

One of my favorite quotes from the spiritual teacher, Eckhart Tolle, is: *"Wherever you are, be there totally."* I've learned to apply this wisdom to my life, and it has helped immeasurably. So often, we are tempted to dwell on either the past (how things were) or the future (how things might be). In doing so, however, we often miss out on the present.

Another one of my favorite quotes is the one above, by American cartoonist Bil Keane. It involves a little play on words, but again, it offers us a valuable pearl of wisdom to help us stay focused on today.

We often look back to times in our past with a longing to return to those good times. And we often look ahead, visualizing a preferred future. Neither of these things is bad, in itself, unless doing so prevents us from being present to the reality of today. Often, in our day-to-day experiences, we might find ourselves wishing we were somewhere else. For example, I can't begin to count the number of times I've found myself in the slow line at a grocery store, or the countless times I've missed a stoplight, causing me to sit and wait for what seems to be an eternity. I've learned to handle these situations with a different perspective.

Whenever I find myself inconvenienced in some way — in line at the Department of Motor Vehicles, in a doctor's office, in a meeting, or waiting for a friend who is late for lunch — I remind myself that wherever I am is exactly where God wants me to be at that particular moment. So I have learned to ask myself "Why?" Why does God want me to be right here right now? Sometimes I'm able to figure it out. Sometimes I'm not. In either case, considering such a thought gives me a new perspective on what might otherwise be a very annoying situation.

I'm grateful for this perspective for two reasons. First, it helps me to be more patient, with myself and with others. Second, it encourages me to seek God's presence in the ordinary experiences of my day. Being "present to the present" is not always easy, but when I make a conscious decision to do so, I find it much easier to "be there totally."

Reflection Questions:

1. How do you cope with the frustration and stress of waiting unexpectedly for someone or some thing?

2. Have you given consideration to the possibility that, when you find yourself delayed or waiting unexpectedly, God has a particular reason for you to be in that particular place at that particular time?

46

The Shadow of Grief

"Part of every misery is, so to speak,
the misery's shadow or reflection:
the fact that you don't merely suffer
but have to keep on thinking about the fact that you suffer.
I not only live each endless day in grief,
but live each day thinking about living each day in grief."
~ C. S. Lewis

In the weeks and months following the unexpected death of my father in 2008, I struggled with an overwhelming sense of loss and disorientation. Not only was I living each day in the shadow of grief, but, as C. S. Lewis mentioned, I was also thinking about the fact that I was having a tough time dealing with the loss. In some ways, living in a culture which seems so preoccupied with getting over life's setbacks as quickly as possible, it was tempting for me to just put my father's death out of my head and move on with my life. I couldn't do that.

While, in some ways, that might have been easier than embracing the process of grief, it was simply not something I was capable of doing. I didn't spend all day every day dwelling on my father's death. I was able to teach my classes without being overly-distracted or preoccupied with my grief. As challenging as it was, however, I made a conscious decision to confront the loss head-on. I read several books about grief, death, and, in particular, the death of one's father. Some of what I read was very practical and inspirational. I also made an effort to talk with other men who had dealt with the death of their father. I found that to be incredibly helpful.

Embracing my grief during that time seemed to keep me closer to my father. I thought about him many times each day. Every day, without exception. I was confident that, over time, things would change and I would be able to get through an entire day without thinking about him, but I wasn't ready to do that in those first few months. I honestly believed that I was honoring my Dad by keeping him present in my thoughts and close to my heart.

Grief is a difficult, yet natural part of living — and loving. I had no desire to just "get over" the pain I was experiencing. I wanted to find a way to integrate my feelings, and the memory of my father, into my life in a healthy way. I wanted to remember who my father was, what he did in his lifetime, and how he influenced the people in his life — especially me.

As I look back on this challenging period in my life, I am able to do so with an incredible sense of gratitude. I have no regrets about embracing my grief and allowing the healing to take place in its own time. There were those few who let me know they thought I was taking too long, but I respectfully ignored them, knowing that many people who fail to do their grief work well find themselves dealing with the loss in less than healthy ways at a later time. I know now, more than ever, that grief is the price we pay for love.

Reflection Questions:

1. When you are coping with the death of a loved one, do you have the need or desire to move on quickly, or are you comfortable

embracing the process of grief, even if it takes longer than others think is necessary?

2. What strategies have you employed, or could you employ, to help you embrace the process of healthy grieving when a loved one dies?

3. Have you experienced, or considered the possibility, that after a period of healthy grieving, a time will come when you will be able to recall your loved one with gratitude, rather than grief?

47

"It's All Good

"Thanks be to God!"
~ Dad

*E*very few years, a word or phrase becomes popular among young people. Many years ago, I recall such words as "keen" and "swell" being used to refer to things or experiences that were favorable. In the mid-1990's, the word "hella" came to be used as an adjective by young people, particularly in Northern California. I quickly learned from my students that the weather outside could be "hella hot" or a reading assignment could be "hella long." I never much liked that word.

"No problem" became a common response to a request for a favor. And as my cousin, Dan, so accurately pointed out in his eulogy at my Dad's funeral, my father's response to so many things in his lifetime was, "Thanks be to God!"

In recent years, another new phrase has emerged among high school and college students: "It's all good." I like this phrase very much.

Life is not perfect. It never is. Yet even when things don't go as planned, or when someone is disappointed with the way something turned out, the phrase "It's all good" allows the conversation to end on a positive note.

It's interesting to note that the phrase has biblical roots. In the story of creation, God created light and saw that it was good. God then created the earth and plants and trees and other types of vegetation, and saw that they were good. God then created the sun and the moon and a variety of living creatures, and acknowledged that they were good. After creating human life, however, God looked at that which had been created and saw that it was *very* good.

Yes, it's all good — not perfect, maybe, but definitely good. It's helpful to remember this when we are confronted with disappointments in life. It's so easy to notice what isn't good, constantly focusing on all the imperfections in the world around us. There are so many things we would like to change or see improved upon in the world, but overall, it really is all good.

I know that, throughout much of my life, I had a tendency to focus on what needed to improve. I often took what was good for granted and paid more attention to the things that were not the way I thought they should be. I didn't necessarily like this about myself, but I knew that's how I was. I tended to be overly-critical of myself and others. It was much too easy for me to see the flaws in things, and in other people.

In recent years, however, I have made a concerted effort to focus on the positive, to focus on what's good about people and situations. Though I often fail, I try to overlook imperfections in others, and to focus on the good in all situations — with gratitude. Like the young people in our world today, I want to be able to say, "It's all good." If I'm able to do so, I have no doubt that the people around me might be inclined to say, "Thanks be to God!"

Reflection Questions:

1. Is it all good? Despite the reality of pain and suffering in our world, do you have a sense that, overall, it's all good?

2. Do you tend to focus on the negative or the positive things happening around you? Are you overly critical or are you compassionately accepting of the flaws of others?

48

Kids Say the Darnedest Things

"Children are not a distraction from more important work.
They are the most important work."
~ C. S. Lewis

In a 2008 *Family Circus* cartoon, little Billy's mother, holding a tattered book in her hands, said to Billy, "This dear old encyclopedia is falling apart, Billy." Billy looked at the old text and replied with absolute seriousness, "Maybe we should call an encyclopediatrician?"

It was the Summer of 1990. I was driving down San Tomas Expressway on our way home to our West San José condominium. My son, Tom, then a four-year-old, was sitting in the front passenger seat of my 1985 Honda Accord. My middle son, Steve, was buckled into his child seat in the back. As we often did when I was in the car with the boys, we were playing the "Alphabet Game." We would start with the letter "A" and each of us would try to think of a word which began with that letter. Tom was pretty good at the game. Steve, then only two-years-old, needed a little help.

We were doing pretty well with the game when we got to the letter "H". Tom gave it a lot of thought, then perked up a bit and blurted out, "Honda!" He was very proud of himself for coming up with the answer.

I complimented him on selecting such a good word. Before we had a chance to move on to the next letter, however, Tom asked me, "This car is a Honda, right?"

"Yes, it is!" I replied.

"Is Mom's car a Honda, too?"

Again, I said, "Yes. It is."

Tom thought for a moment before speaking. "But Mom's car is smaller than your car," he observed.

"Yes," I said. "This is a Honda Accord. Mom drives a Honda Civic. It's a little smaller."

Tom processed this information for a brief time. Then, with absolute seriousness, inquired, "Is Mom's car a Hondaminium?"

There are so many wonderful memories I have of my sons' early years. I cherish these memories with gratitude. This story certainly stands out as one of the more humorous conversations I enjoyed with them.

Reflection Questions:

1. What memories do you have of your own childhood, or that of your children, which are a source of joy and gratitude for you?

2. When have you been pleasantly surprised by the innocent words of a young child?

49

Eight O'Clock

"A mother's love is a blessing..."
~ Traditional Irish Ballad

After living in San Francisco for the first eighteen yeas of my life, I moved out of my family home in August 1972 and relocated to the Santa Clara Valley to begin college. For the first two years, I might have called home to speak with my parents once or twice a month, just to say hello. I certainly would not have wanted to give them the impression that I wasn't totally independent. I didn't own a phone, so I relied on a pay phone in the hallway of the dormitory at Bellarmine College Prep, where I was living and working at the time. I continued living at Bellarmine for those first two summers, as well.

In late August 1974, I moved to Nassau, in the Bahamas, where I had accepted a teaching position at Saint Augustine's College. I lived in one of the guest rooms of the Saint Augustine's Monastery, perched on a hill above the school campus. When I called my parents, which I did rarely that year, I had to walk over to the monastery kitchen to use the phone there. I'll admit, I did experience a bit of homesickness in my first semester in Nassau, but the cost of calling home was prohibitive, so my usual means of communication with my parents was by postal mail.

When I returned to the Santa Clara Valley, I lived and worked in the dormitory at Bellarmine Prep for another three years. As I had done previously, I relied on the hallway pay phone to call home. I kept rolls of quarters handy to insert into the coin slot every three minutes or so to continue the conversation. As was the case in my first two years of college, one or two calls per month seemed to keep everyone happy.

Even after Kathy and I married, calls to my parents in The City from our home in Santa Clara were weekly, at best. We had our hands full raising our boys, and I mistakenly believed that my parents had better things to do with their time than talk to me on the phone. Things changed, however, after my Dad died.

In the days and weeks following my Dad's services, calls to my Mom ended with her saying, "Okay, I'll talk to you tomorrow." At first, I thought... tomorrow? It didn't take long for me to realize that, yes, Mom meant tomorrow!

Since that time, I have called my Mom almost every night. My two sisters do the same. Even my brother, a Jesuit priest living and working in Rome, calls Mom every morning, which is right around dinner time in Rome. I usually make my call around 8:00 p.m.

While some might think I am fulfilling some type of unreasonable parental obligation, I know that's not the case. I'm embracing a tremendous gift. Many of my friends don't have the opportunity to call their mother any more. I'm well aware of this. So, for me, having the opportunity to do so every night is an experience I cherish.

As the old Irish ballad states so clearly, *"A mother's love is a blessing..."* It most certainly is. It's a blessing for which I am especially grateful.

Reflection Questions:

1. Is there anyone in your life — a parent, grandparent, child, friend, or neighbor — who might appreciate a phone call from you now and then?

2. Have you ever taken someone for granted in such a way that, only after their death, you came to realize how special it might have been to maintain regular communication with them?

50

Just Let It Go

> *"It is the mark of an educated mind*
> *to be able to entertain a thought*
> *without accepting it."*
> ~ Aristotle

The experience, I would think, is fairly common. You're driving down the road with a friend, or, perhaps, having a conversation with a coworker over lunch, when you make a statement which, in your opinion, is factual. The other person responds by disagreeing with you and offering an alternative fact, with a tone of certainty equal to your own. Both cannot be correct. In some cases you may be 100% certain that your statement is accurate. At other times, you're open to the possibility that, just maybe, you might be mistaken. In this case, however, you have no doubt. You are right. Your friend or coworker is wrong. What do you do?

For much of my life, I had an insatiable need to prove people wrong. Not that I was always right, but when I was absolutely certain of the validity of my statement, and someone disagreed with me, I wanted to make certain that they knew I was right. Not surprisingly, even when I provided irrefutable evidence to support my claim, and the person was duly corrected, I experienced a feeling of emptiness. Rarely, if ever, was there any tangible sense of victory or accomplishment in doing so.

It took awhile — I can sometimes be a slow learner — but, in time, I learned that being right is far less important than being kind and respectful. I have found tremendous value in responding to the other person with the words, "Hmmm… I could be wrong," even when I firmly believe I'm right. Really, what difference does it make if I'm right or wrong? Which is of greater value, the accurateness of one's statements or the quality of one's relationships?

I had the pleasure of meeting John Wooden in the summer of 1974. Wooden was the legendary UCLA men's basketball coach who led the Bruins to ten NCAA championships in twelve years. Those ten teams recorded a combined total of 291 wins and only 10 losses. Wooden always considered himself to be a teacher, on and off the court. One pearl of wisdom he shared addressed the issue of disagreements between individuals. He said, *"We can agree to disagree, but we don't need to be disagreeable."*

When we agree to disagree, we send a clear message that our relationship is more important than our opinion, regardless of how confident we might be in what we've said.

Bishop Desmond Tutu also weighed-in on this topic: *"Our maturity will be judged by how well we are able to agree to disagree and yet continue to love one another, to care for one another, to cherish one another, and seek the greater good of the other."* To seek the greater good of the other — is this not a wonderful definition of the word "love"?

I read the following quote on a friend's Facebook page recently: *"I'd agree with you, but then we'd both be wrong."* Yes, there is some humor in this statement, but only if it's spoken with clearly-understood sarcasm, rather than absolute sincerity.

Most people have a desire to be right. Others have a need be right. There is a difference. The ability to agree to disagree, whether that option is verbalized or not, respects the relationship, and the person with whom you have that relationship. It's certainly a better option, I would think, than ending any conversation with the dismissing words, "Yeah,.... whatever!"

Reflection Questions:

1. How do you cope with the situation when someone disagrees with a statement you make which you are absolutely certain is factually accurate?

2. In what other ways can we exhibit our desire for our relationships to take priority over acceptance of our opinions by others?

CONCLUSION

"Most of us suffer from a huge gratitude gap.
We know we should be grateful,
but something holds us back."
~ Janice Kaplan

Gratitude works! It is both magical and contagious, but it doesn't happen by itself. It takes desire, a bit of self-discipline, and a little time to develop the habit of experiencing life through the lens of gratitude. A moment's pause for gratitude is all we need each day to begin to live our lives with a genuine *attitude of gratitude*.

Once we begin to embrace gratefulness, we are invited — and challenged — to take the next step: to express our gratitude to others. There are so many ways we can do this. A phone call, a handwritten note of gratitude, a simple e-mail message, a personal visit, a plate of home-baked cookies, a bouquet of flowers, a random act of kindness,... The possibilities are endless. In the end, it's a win-win situation. The person being thanked will feel better and YOU will feel better, too. That's how gratitude works.

The ball is in our court!

ABOUT THE AUTHOR

Kevin Carroll was born and raised in San Francisco, California. He is a graduate of Saint Ignatius College Preparatory, Santa Clara University (B.A. in English/Writing), and the University of San Francisco (M.A. in Education). After a forty-year career in education and pastoral ministry, Kevin retired in June 2015 to pursue a second career in writing.

Kevin, and his wife Kathy, currently live in San José, California. They have three sons and two adorable grandchildren, Liam and Emily.

When he is not writing or playing with his grandkids, Kevin enjoys reading and spending time outdoors. He has been inspired by the writings of Paulo Coelho, Coach John Wooden, Roland Merullo, Hal Urban, Janice Kaplan, Harold Ivan Smith, Jack London, Father Jim Martin, S.J., Frank McCourt, and many more accomplished authors.

A Moment's Pause for Gratitude is Kevin's first published book.

Printed in the United States
By Bookmasters